THE LITTLE BOOK OF

BIG

517 *Ways to Stretch,*

Color Die
p. 240

BRAIN

Strengthen and Grow Your Brain

GAMES

by IVAN MOSCOVICH

illustrated by TIM ROBINSON

WORKMAN PUBLISHING · NEW YORK

P9-CKF-016

Library of Congress Cataloging-in-Publication Data is available.

ISBN 978-0-7611-6173-8

Workman books are available at special discounts when purchased in
bulk for premiums and sales promotions as well as for fund-raising or
educational use. Special editions or book excerpts also can be created
to specification. For details, contact the Special Sales Director at the
address below, or send an email to specialmarkets@workman.com.

Design by Bob Perino

PlayThink 184, "Sharing Cakes," and PlayThink 178, "Japanese Temple
Problem from 1844," from *Which Way Did the Bicycle Go?*, by Joseph
D.E. Konhauser, Dan Velleman, and Stan Wagon. Reprinted by
permission from The Mathematical Association of America, *Which
Way Did the Bicycle Go?* pages 62 and 107.

Workman Publishing Company, Inc.
225 Varick Street
New York, NY 10014-4381
workman.com

WORKMAN is a registered trademark of
Workman Publishing Co., Inc.

Printed in China

First printing October 2010

10

Contents

Introduction

I love games. Over the last forty years I have collected, designed and invented thousands upon thousands of them. One of the reasons I'm so passionate about games is that I believe they can change the way people think. They can allow us to see the world in new ways. They can remind us to have fun.

Psychologists have long known that children learn about the world through play; now it is clear that adults can also benefit from games. Even as we age, our brains continue to form neurons and make new connections. In order to encourage this growth, research has shown you need to exercise your brain as you would a muscle—constantly challenging it in new and different ways. As puzzlemaster Nob Yoshigahara once said: "What jogging is to the body, thinking is to the brain. The more we do it, the better we become."

Playing games is a truly important activity. We can understand the most abstract and difficult concepts if we allow ourselves the luxury of approaching them not as work, but as fun—and as a form of exploration. In this way, puzzles are an ideal way to have fun while stretching and strengthening your brain. And the more diverse the challenges are, the better your workout.

For that reason, I've chosen activities that span many topics and combine entertainment and brain-teasing. Some of the puzzles are completely original, while others are novel adaptations of classic and modern challenges. Because they transcend puzzles and games in the traditional sense, I have given them a new name: PlayThinks. Whatever its form, a PlayThink will ideally transfer you to a state of mind where play and problem solving coexist. It will stimulate creative thinking and push your brain to grow in new directions. My goal is for you to play the games, solve the problems and come away more curious, more inventive, more intuitive.

How to Use This Book

The puzzles I like best are not always the hardest. Sometimes a puzzle that is quite easy to solve is elegant enough to make it especially satisfying. Solving puzzles has as much to do with the way you think about them as with natural ability or some impersonal measure of intelligence. Most people should be able to solve all the problems in this book, although some problems will undoubtedly seem easier than others.

The puzzles in this book are designed to permit easy access to many ideas, in different contexts and at different levels. They are organized into chapters according to the ideas they center around—probability, say, or patterns. You may find that by attacking the PlayThinks in order; you can build an understanding of a field of knowledge, but that is far from the only way to use this book.

Each PlayThink is rated in difficulty from 1 to 10. You might decide to do all the puzzles rated 1 and 2, then try the ones rated 3 and 4, and thus build up your abilities as a problem solver. Or you might jump around in the book, first taking on the subjects that interest you most until you are ready to work your way deeper into the frontiers of what you think you don't know.

You get the idea: it's all up to you. Just don't forget to play. Enjoy!

—Ivan Moscovich

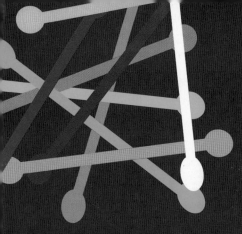

Thinking about PlayThinks

This book is really all about think-ing. In solving puzzles, comprehension is at least as important as visual perception or mathe-matical knowledge. This chapter will introduce you to problems that will stretch your imagination and improve your creativity, insight, and intuition. Thinking is a learnable skill, like cooking or golf. If you make even a small effort to develop it, you will see improvement.

HALVING SEVEN

Can you prove that seven is half of twelve?

$$7 + 7 = 12?$$

AHMES'S PUZZLE

Seven houses each have seven cats. Each cat kills seven mice. Each of the mice, if alive, would have eaten seven ears of wheat. Each ear of wheat produces seven measures of flour.

How many measures of flour were saved by the cats?

3

NESTING FRAMES

I saw this giant minimalist outdoor sculpture in a garden. The three nesting frames are intertwined so that the frame marked with red is inside the frame marked in yellow, which is inside the frame marked in blue. But curiously enough, the frame marked in blue is inside the frame marked in red!

Can you figure out the relative sizes of the three frames?

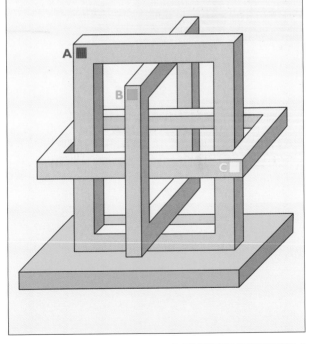

FLAP DOOR

Study for a moment the drawing of the flap door. Now cover it and look at the drawings at the bottom. From memory can you choose the correct shape of the door?

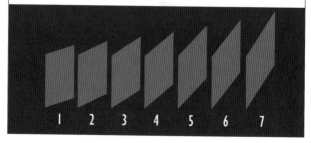

1   2   3   4   5   6   7

DIFFICULTY: ●●●●●○○○○○
COMPLETION: ☐ TIME: _____

CHICKEN OR EGG?

Can you answer the ancient question: Which came first, the chicken or the egg?

6

DIFFICULTY: ●●●●●○○○○○
COMPLETION: ☐ TIME: _____

TOY MATTERS

Each toy has a price, and the sum totals for each row and column are given, except for the last row and column. Can you work out the missing sums and determine the price for each toy?

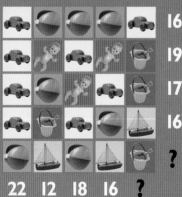

7

PICK-UP STICKS I

This puzzle works just like the familiar children's game. Remove one stick at a time from the pile, making sure that no other stick lies on top of it. To clear the entire pile, what color sequence must be chosen?

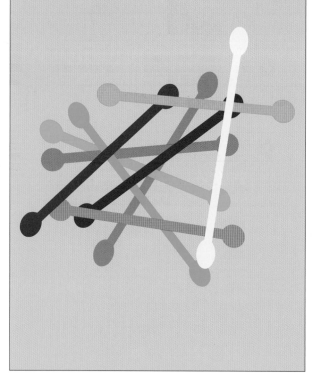

DIFFICULTY: ●●●●●○○○○○
COMPLETION: ☐ TIME: _____

MATCH SQUARES

Twenty-four matchsticks can be arranged to create the pattern illustrated to the right. Can you remove eight matchsticks from the configuration so that you are left with two squares that do not touch each other?

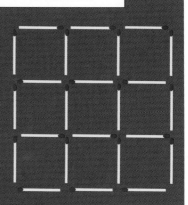

DIFFICULTY: ●●●●●●○○○○
COMPLETION: ☐ TIME: _____

LOTTERY DRAW

If you draw the lucky ticket, you win the lottery jackpot. You are given the option to draw one ticket out of a box of 10, or draw ten times out of a box of 100. Which choice gives you the best odds?

10

DIFFICULTY: ●●●●●●●○○○
COMPLETION: ☐ TIME: ______

PATTERN 15

Five different whole numbers add up to 15. Multiply those same five numbers together, and the result is 120.

Can you determine what those five numbers are?

$$\square + \square + \square + \square + \square = 15$$

$$\square \quad \square \quad \square \quad \square \quad \square = 120$$

11

DIFFICULTY: ●●●●●●●●○○
COMPLETION: ☐ TIME: ______

PATTERN 30

Five different single-digit whole numbers add up to 30. Two of them are given as 1 and 8.

Multiply those same five numbers together, and the result is 2,520.

Can you determine what the other three numbers are?

$$\square + \square + \square + 1 + 8 = 30$$

$$\square \times \square \times \square \times 1 \times 8 = 2{,}520$$

12

DIFFICULTY: ●●●●○○○○○○○○
COMPLETION: ☐ TIME: _____

IMPOSSIBLE DOMINO BRIDGE

At first glance this structure seems impossible to build. After all, it would collapse before many of the dominoes were laid. But the bridge is actually simple to construct if you approach it with the right frame of mind. Can you determine how to do it?

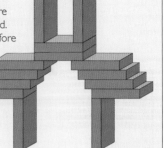

13

DIFFICULTY: ●●●●●●○○○○○○
COMPLETION: ☐ TIME: _____

GLOVES IN THE DARK

There are twenty-two gloves in a drawer: five pairs of red gloves, four pairs of yellow and two pairs of green. If the lights are out and you must select the gloves in the dark, how many must you choose to ensure that you have at least one matching pair?

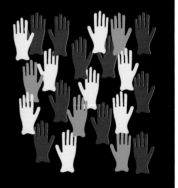

OVERLAPPING SQUARES

Can you fit the six squares on the right into the big gray square below to create a pattern of eighteen squares of four different sizes formed by their outlines? The white grid lines are provided only to help in the alignment of the overlapping squares.

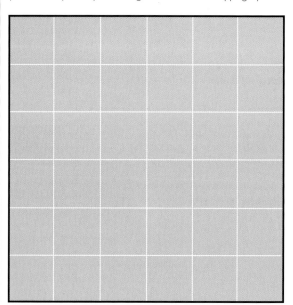

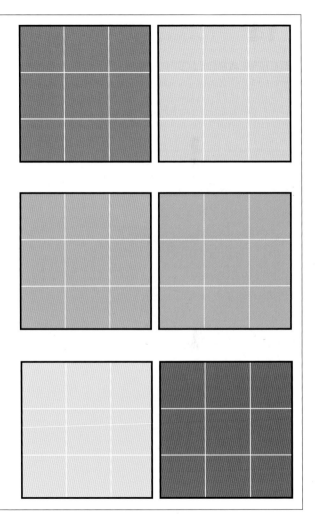

15

DIFFICULTY: ●●●●●●●●○○
COMPLETION: ☐ TIME: _____

ALIEN ABDUCTION

Four UFOs hover above a man they plan to abduct. To catch the man, the four aliens must create a rectangular energy field around him. Each alien fires a laser randomly, either to the left of the man or to his right. Out of all the possible random combinations of the four laser shots, what is the probability that each will form a side of a rectangle around the man? (In the example shown, all rays are directed to the right of the man.)

16

BOOKWORM

A bookworm finds itself on page 1 of volume 1 and begins eating straight through to the last page of volume 5. If each book is 6 centimeters thick, including the front and back covers, which are half a centimeter each, what is the distance the bookworm travels?

17

HALLOWEEN MASK

You have five different colors of paint. How many different ways can you paint the Halloween mask if you make the eyes, nose and mouth each a different color?

TREASURE ISLAND

To confuse his enemies, the pirate who made this map made only one of the statements false. Can you still figure out where the treasure is buried?

THREE-COIN FLIP

You ask a friend about probability, and he tells you the following: "The odds of three tossed coins turning up all heads or all tails is one in two, that is, fifty-fifty. That's because anytime you toss three coins, at least two must match, either two heads or two tails. So that means the third coin—which is equally likely to be heads or tails—determines the odds."

Is your friend right? If not, what are the odds of three tossed coins turning up all heads or all tails?

SCRAMBLED MATCHSTICKS

It takes just a couple of little twists to turn these matchsticks into a message. Can you find the word?

21

DIFFICULTY: ●●●●●○○○○○
COMPLETION: ☐ TIME: _____

HOG-TIED

Two hostages are tied together by their wrists, as shown. Can they separate themselves without cutting the rope or untying the knots?

22

DIFFICULTY: ●●●●●●●○○○
COMPLETION: ☐ TIME: _____

SIX–SEVEN

Is there a way to use three 6s to make a 7?

23

DIFFICULTY: ●●●●●○○○○○
COMPLETION: ☐ TIME: _____

RIDDLE OF THE SPHINX

Can you solve one of the greatest puzzles of antiquity?

In Greek mythology the Sphinx was a monster who possessed the head of a woman, the body of a lion and the wings of an eagle. The Sphinx guarded the gates of the city of Thebes, challenging all who would enter with this simple riddle:

"What goes on four legs in the morning, on two legs at noon, and on three legs at dusk?"

The Sphinx killed anyone who could not answer the riddle and vowed to destroy herself should anyone solve it. She had to make good on her word when Oedipus told her the answer. Can you?

24

DIFFICULTY: ●●●●●○○○○○
COMPLETION: ☐ TIME: _____

PACKING SWORD

A soldier needs to store his 70-centimeter-long sword, but the only chest available measures 40 centimeters long, 30 centimeters wide and 50 centimeters high. Will the sword fit in the chest?

ODD INTERSECTION

The red closed line is drawn so that it crosses a black closed line from inside to outside or vice versa exactly ten times.

Can you draw a new red closed line over the same black line so that it makes only nine crossings?

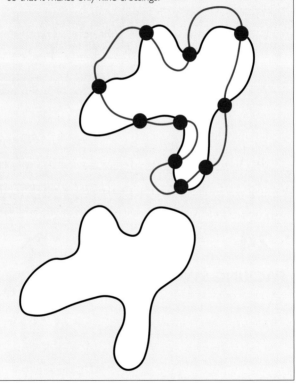

26

LADYBUG RENDEZVOUS

Mister Ladybug meets Miss Ladybug on the petal of a flower.

"I'm a boy," says the one with red dots. "I'm a girl," says the one with yellow dots.

Then they both laugh because at least one of them is lying. From that information can you tell which one has the red dots and which has the yellow?

27

OVERLAPPING RUGS

A square rug that is 2 meters on a side overlaps a smaller square rug that is only 1 meter on a side. The corner of the larger rug falls exactly on the center of the smaller one. Not counting the fringe, what percentage of the smaller rug is hidden?

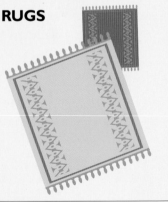

28

DIFFICULTY: ●●●○○○○○○○
COMPLETION: ☐ TIME: _____

HANDSHAKES I

At a business meeting each person shook hands with every other person exactly once. If there were fifteen handshakes, can you tell how many people attended the meeting?

29

DIFFICULTY: ●●●●○○○○○○
COMPLETION: ☐ TIME: _____

HANDSHAKES 2

Six people are sitting at a round table. How many combinations of simultaneous, noncrossing handshakes are possible?

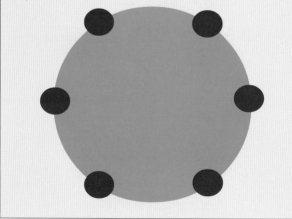

PHONE NUMBER

A man and a woman meet at a bar. After a long conversation they agree to have dinner the next day if the man remembers to call the woman to confirm the date. The next morning the man discovers that he can remember the digits in her number—2, 3, 4, 5, 6, 7 and 8—but he has completely forgotten their order.

If he decides to arrange the seven digits in random order and dial every combination, what are the chances that any given phone number will be hers?

MISSING FRACTIONS

Can you determine the logic to the pattern and use that knowledge to fill in the missing squares?

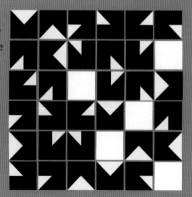

LAST MAN

Imagine you are the editor at a science fiction magazine and you read the following lines at the beginning of a story:

"The last man on earth sat alone in his room. Suddenly there was a knock at the door!"

Can you change one word in the first sentence to make the man's isolation before the knock at the door more complete?

FRUIT BASKETS

A market displays three fruit baskets, each with the correct price. Let's say you want just one banana, one orange and one apple. Can you work out what the price would be?

$1.45 $1.30 $1.30

34

DIFFICULTY: ●●●●●●●●○○○
COMPLETION: ☐ TIME: _____

FAULT-FREE SQUARE

The manner in which the one-by-two bricks were packed into a square has created a so-called fault line—a straight line of edges that runs from one side to the other. To create a stronger structure, can you repack the bricks into the square so that it is free of faults?

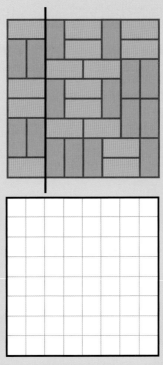

35

DIFFICULTY: ●●●●●●●○○○
COMPLETION: ☐ TIME: _____

HOTEL KEYS

A porter leads eight guests to their hotel rooms, rooms 1 through 8. Unfortunately, the keys are unlabeled and the porter has mixed up their order. Using trial and error, what is the maximum number of attempts the porter must make before he opens all the doors?

36

DIFFICULTY: ●●●●●●●○○○
COMPLETION: ☐ TIME: _____

NETWORK OF TWOS

How many numbers can you write using three 2s and no other symbols?

37

FASHION SHOW

Three models—Miss Pink, Miss Green and Miss Blue—are on the catwalk. Their dresses are solid pink, solid green and solid blue.

"It's strange," Miss Blue remarks to the others. "We are named Pink, Green and Blue, and our dresses are pink, green and blue, but none of us is wearing the dress that matches her name."

"That is a coincidence," says the woman in green.

From that information, can you determine the color of each model's dress?

38

PIGGY BANKS

Three nickels and three dimes are distributed among three piggy banks so that each bank holds two coins. Although each bank has a number of cents printed on its side, all three banks are mislabeled. Is it possible to determine how to correctly relabel the banks simply by shaking one of the banks until one of the coins drops out? If so, explain how.

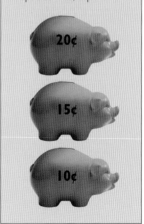

COLOR CARDS

Which of the four numbered cards has a pattern that is not found in the colored grid below?

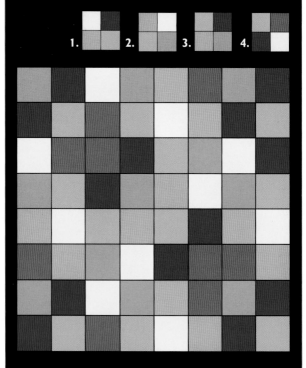

1.　　2.　　3.　　4.

PYRAMID ART SCULPTURE

Four cloth sails are fixed to the wire structure of a three-dimensional sculpture, as shown. What pattern do you see when you look down on the sculpture from above?

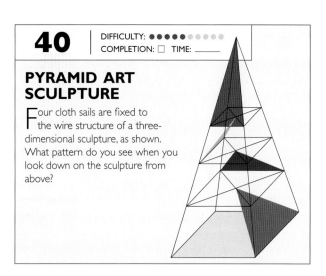

STAR STRIPS

Can you make a perfect star from three identical strips of translucent paper?

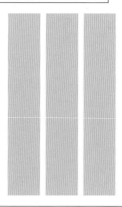

42

DIFFICULTY: ●●●●●●●●●○○○○
COMPLETION: □ TIME: _____

GOLD BAR

This gold bar is exactly 31 centimeters long. If you want to divide the bar into smaller segments so that one or a combination of segments can add up to every whole number of centimeters from 1 to 31, how many cuts must you make?

43

DIFFICULTY: ●●●●●○○○○○
COMPLETION: □ TIME: _____

MATCHSTICK TRIANGLES

Starting with the equilateral triangle shown, can you create two smaller equilateral triangles by moving just four matchsticks?

Then can you create four even smaller equilateral triangles by moving just four matchsticks?

KNIGHTS ATTACK

Twenty knights are placed on a chessboard so that each one can attack one and only one other knight. (As you know, the knights move in an L-shaped manner, two squares up and one square over, or two squares over and one square up.) Is it possible to pack even more knights on the board and still follow the one-attack rule?

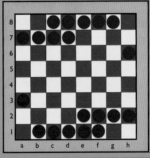

45

HAT MIX

Three men check their hats at the theater, but the attendant mixes up the checks as she hands them out. When the three men return after the performance to claim their hats, what are the chances that they all will have their own hats returned to them?

46

FACTORS

At the chalkboard the teacher demonstrates the four factors of the number 6—that is, the whole numbers that can divide into 6 and leave no remainder. (Remember, a number is always its own factor, as is 1.) Between 1 and 100, there are five numbers that have exactly twelve factors. How quickly can you find all five?

NECKLACE PAIRS

Can you place beads on the necklace so that each two-color pair shown at left appears exactly once in either direction?

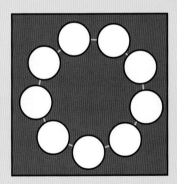

TRAVERSING SQUARES

Can you trace a path along all five yellow squares without picking up your pencil, going over the same segment twice or crossing a line you've already laid down?

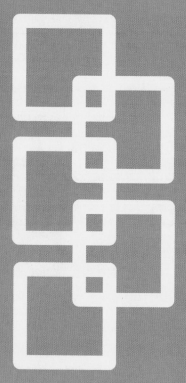

2

Geometry

G **eometry allows us to analyze** the size, shape, and position of objects in space. In this chapter, you'll explore some of the building blocks of this ancient form of mathematics by solving puzzles of symmetry—the ability to be reflected across or rotated about an axis without appearing different—and shifting shapes in space.

SHADOW GARDEN

All twelve walls of a dodecagonal garden are illuminated by a single lamp, which is positioned in the garden's center. Can you redesign the garden so that even though a lamp is placed at its center, each of the twelve walls is partly or entirely in shadow? The walls must be straight, but they don't have to be the same length.

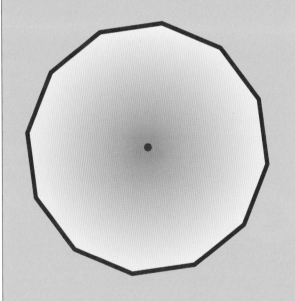

50

TAXICAB ROUTES

Imagine you drive a taxicab in Gridlock City. Your cab is called to visit three places in succession and return back to the garage. The points on the map are marked 1 for the garage and 2, 3 and 4 for the pickup points. Can you find the shortest route that will accomplish this task? Are there alternative routes you could take?

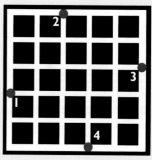

51

FLATLAND HIERARCHY

In *Flatland,* Edwin Abbott describes a society of geometric shapes subject to a strict hierarchy. Ladies are sharp straight lines; soldiers and workmen are isosceles triangles; middle-class people are equilateral triangles; professionals are either squares or pentagons; the wealthy are hexagons; and the top of the class system—the high priests—are circles.

Of course, since ladies are one-dimensional lines, they are invisible from some directions and may be hazardous to run into. How do you think the Flatlanders avoid this problem?

BLUEPRINT AND SOLIDS

For each group of objects, can you find the one that was constructed by folding the pattern provided?

MULTIVIEWS

Imagine flying over a city in an airplane. As seen from above, the buildings seem quite different from the way they look when you are standing in front of them. And yet nothing about the buildings has changed. This is the concept that architects tap into when they represent their building plans in two different ways: the plan, which represents the way the building will be laid out on the ground, and the front elevation, which is derived directly from the plans to represent the way the building will look from the front. A third type of architectural drawing, the perspective, combines those two views to create a more realistic view of the building.

This puzzle is based on the same concept. There are sixteen objects, yet seen from the front, they present only four different types of views. And seen from the top, they present four different types of views. But every object with a similar front view has a different overhead view—sixteen unique objects.

Can you match each object with its proper overhead and front views? Write your answers in the boxes provided.

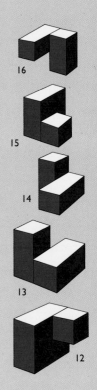

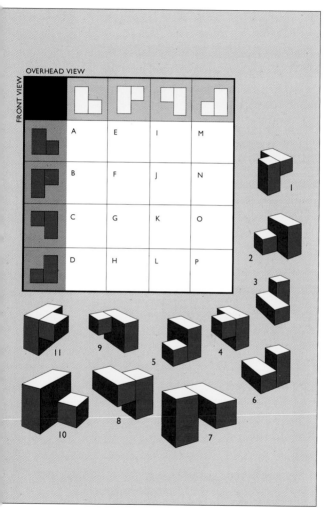

SYMMETRICAL FLOOR

This floor is made of identical square tiles, each of which is diagonally divided into red and yellow. If the floor is symmetrical about the red axes, can you fill in the rest of the tiles to find the overall pattern?

DIFFICULTY: ●●●●●●●●●●●●
COMPLETION: ☐ TIME: _____

REFLECTION-REVERSAL

In each row the tiles in this pattern are supposed to be the reflected and inverted image of the tiles to their left. That is, the colors are to be reversed and the tile flipped along the vertical axis. Which tile does not follow that rule?

56

DIFFICULTY: ●●●●●●●●●●●●
COMPLETION: ☐ TIME: _____

ALPHABET I

What do the red letters have in common? What do the blue letters have in common?

ALPHABET 2

What's the difference between the red letters and the blue letters?

HFOJI
GXL

MYSTERY SIGNS

Can you decipher the mystery signs and read the secret word? A small mirror may help if you're stumped.

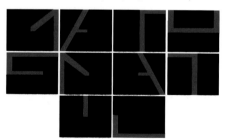

SYMMETRY AXES

Symmetrical patterns can be found by folding and cutting paper or by using a plane mirror. For each of the thirteen shapes shown below, find and draw the symmetry axes. Are some figures not symmetrical? Which shape has the most symmetry axes?

60

DIFFICULTY: ●●●○○○○○○○
COMPLETION: ☐ TIME: ______

SYMMETRY ALPHABET

Can you draw the symmetry axes for the capital letters of the alphabet? If the letter is rotationally symmetrical, draw the point of rotation. Leave asymmetrical letters unmarked.

A B C D

E F G H

I J K L

M N O

P Q R S

T U V W

X Y Z

ALPHABET 3

What is the difference between the red letters and the blue letters?

N P S R Z Q

SYMMETRY OF THE CUBE

The cube has many more rotational symmetries than a two-dimensional figure. Can you find them all?

SYMMETRY SQUARES

Both of these images are symmetrical—but some of the squares have been erased.

In the top image, by carefully observing the position of the black squares in relation to the red line, which is the axis of vertical symmetry, you should be able to fill in the rest of the picture.

In the bottom image, by carefully observing the position of the blue squares in relation to the two red lines, which are the axes of vertical and horizontal symmetry, you should be able to fill in the rest of the picture.

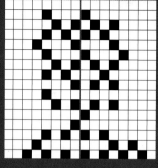

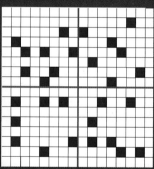

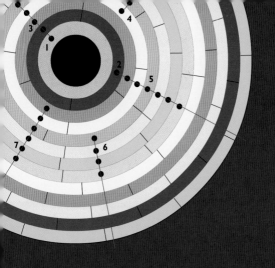

3

Points and Lines

Points are not just marks—they are abstract symbols that define position. And lines are not only the fundamental elements of drawn images but also mathematical symbols that link points, indicate distance, and direction and define space. This chapter will challenge you to see points and lines—and the relationship between them—in a new way.

64

THE SIX-LINE PROBLEM

The six lines in the figure to the right enclose eight triangles of three different sizes. Can you devise a way to draw six straight lines so that they enclose eight triangles of only two different sizes?

65

LINES AND TRIANGLES

With three lines you can enclose one triangle; with four lines, four triangles. Can you enclose ten triangles by adding two more straight lines to the three shown here?

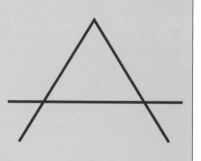

KOBON TRIANGLES I

How many nonoverlapping triangles can you form by drawing six continuous straight lines? Can you do better than this example?

3 lines   4 lines   5 lines

PAPPUS'S THEOREM

Two lines are drawn, and three points are randomly selected on each line. Straight lines connect the six points, and the three intersections of those lines are marked.

Oddly, the three intersections all lie upon a straight line. Will this be true in all cases?

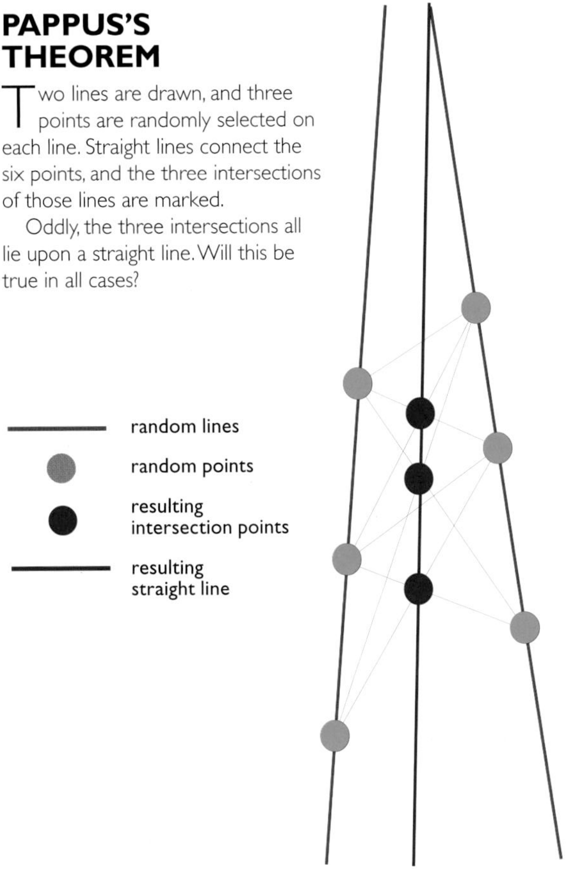

———— random lines

● random points

● resulting intersection points

———— resulting straight line

68

MYSTERY WHEELS

These straight colored lines have been taped to a turntable. When the turntable revolves, the lines will blur into new patterns. Can you envision what each of the four patterns will look like?

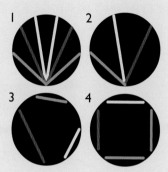

69

CHEESE CUT

Can you cut this wheel of cheese into eight identical pieces with only three straight cuts?

KOBON TRIANGLES 2

How many nonoverlapping triangles can be enclosed by seven straight lines? The illustration shows a six-triangle solution. Can you do better?

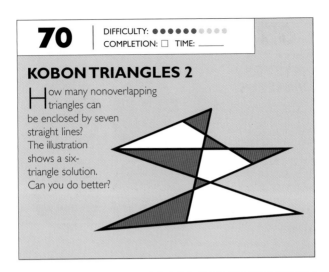

KOBON TRIANGLES 3

How many nonoverlapping triangles can be enclosed by eight straight lines? The illustration shows a six-triangle solution. Can you do better?

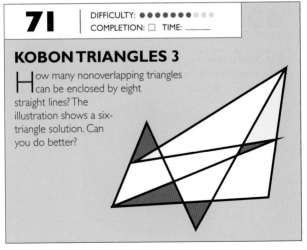

CONVEX OR SIMPLE?

A convex polygon is one in which every point in the interior can be connected to any point on the perimeter with a straight line that does not cross the perimeter. A simple polygon is one in which no lines or sides cross each other. Working with that basic information, can you figure out how many convex polygons are shown in the drawing below?

One of the lines or polygons depicted is different from all the others. Can you tell which one it is?

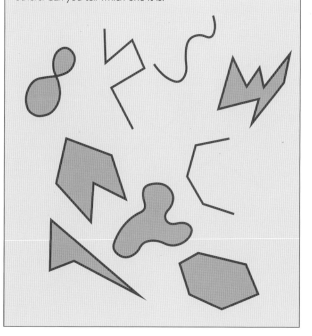

GREAT DIVIDE I

Four straight cuts can divide a cake into ten pieces, as shown below. Is it possible to go one better and divide the cake into eleven pieces?

Can you determine the general rule for finding the greatest number of regions that can be formed by a given number of straight cuts in a single plane?

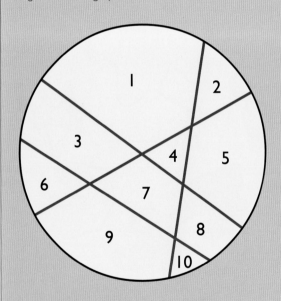

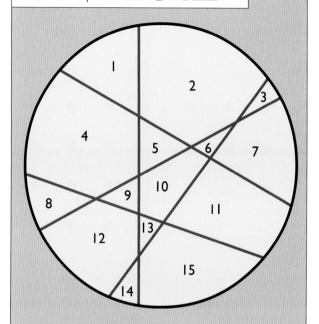

GREAT DIVIDE 2

Five straight cuts are used to cut a cake into fifteen pieces. Can you cut the cake into sixteen pieces with only five cuts?

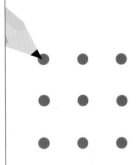

NINE-POINT PROBLEM

Can you connect the nine points with four straight lines without lifting your pencil?

Can you solve this problem using only three straight lines?

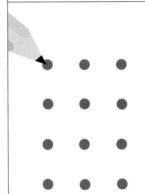

TWELVE-POINT PROBLEM

Can you connect these twelve dots with a series of straight lines without lifting your pencil? What is the least number of lines necessary?

CROSSED BOX

A ten-by-fourteen box is divided into 140 one-by-one compartments. A laser beam shines from the lower left-hand corner of the box to the top right-hand corner.

Without counting, can you work out how many compartments the laser will pass through?

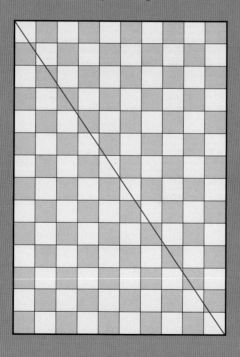

DIFFICULTY: ●●●●●●○○○○
COMPLETION: ☐ TIME: _____

LADYBUGS IN THE FIELD

Drawing just four straight lines across the circle, can you separate the eleven ladybugs into eleven individual compartments?

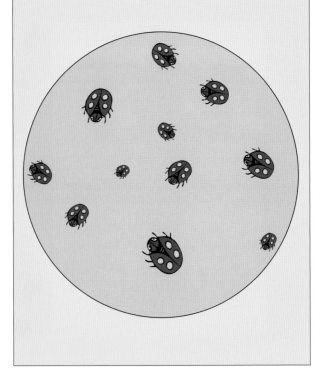

79

DOG TIED

Fido the dog is tied to a tree with a ten-foot length of rope. He wants to get to his doggie bowl, which is fifteen feet away. So Fido trots over and starts eating.

There are no tricks— the rope didn't break and the tree didn't bend. Nothing of that sort. So how did Fido do it?

80

EQUIDISTANT TREES

These three trees are equidistant—that is, each is at an equal distance from every other tree. Is this the maximum number of trees that can be equidistant?

PIXEL CRAFT

Study the two grid patterns below. Can you determine what the image would be if the two patterns were fused together?

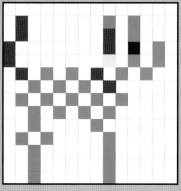

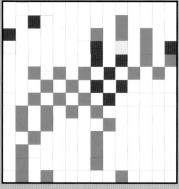

LONGEST LINE

Can you find the longest line connecting two points on the two intersecting circles that passes through the point marked A? (Points A and D are the points at which the two circles intersect.)

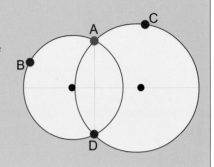

SERPENTS

There are nine snakes—three red, three green and three blue—coiled in closed loops under a rock. The snakes do not touch one another, nor do their loops intersect.

Eight of the snakes are partly uncovered. Just by studying the image, can you tell what color snake is fully hidden by the rock?

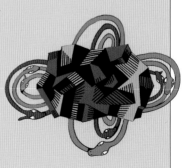

84

PLANTING SIX TREES

A garden is planted with five trees along six straight paths—two paths have three trees, and four paths have two trees. Can you design a new garden with six trees and four paths so that each path has exactly three trees?

85

DIFFICULTY: ●●●●●●●●○○○
COMPLETION: ☐ TIME: _____

TWO-DISTANCE SETS

Points on a plane can be any distance apart. But there is a limited set of points that are exactly one or two discrete distances from every other point in the set. For example, two given points are exactly one distance from each other, and each of the three points that form the vertices of an equilateral triangle are also the same distance from the other two points. Those two sets of points are the only one-distance sets.

An isosceles triangle is an example of a two-distance set. Within a plane, how many other two-distance sets can you find?

one-
distance
sets

two-
distance
set

86

DIFFICULTY: ●●●●●●●●○○○
COMPLETION: ☐ TIME: _____

THREE-DISTANCE SETS

The four points shown below are connected by six lines, each of a different length. This is an example of a six-distance set.

Can you arrange four points so that the interconnections form only three different, discrete distances—one distance three times, one distance twice, and one distance only once? How many examples of this sort of three-distance set can you find?

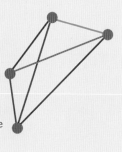

ROWS OF ROSES

M r. Rose wanted to plant sixteen rose-bushes in his garden, and he began to plan how he wanted them laid out. At first he designed his rose garden so that there would be four rows of four roses each, which would result in ten straight lines—four vertical lines, four horizontal lines and two diagonal lines—each of which would have four bushes.

Then Mr. Rose hit on an even better plan: he would plant the sixteen bushes along fifteen straight lines with four bushes in each line. Can you figure out how he planted them?

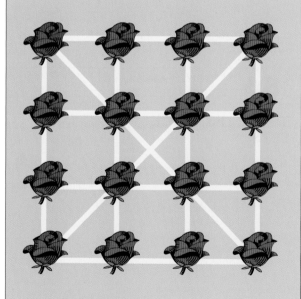

88

DIFFICULTY: ●●●●●○○○○○
COMPLETION: □ TIME: _____

CHERRY IN THE GLASS

Can you empty the glass and remove the cherry by moving just two matchsticks?

(In your solution the glass must retain its original shape.)

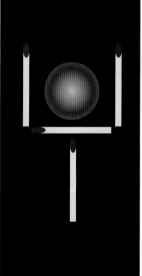

89

DIFFICULTY: ●●●●○○○○○○
COMPLETION: □ TIME: _____

MATCH FISH

Can you change the direction of the fish by moving just three matchsticks?

MATCH CONFIGURATIONS

This puzzle is based on an old solitaire game. How many topologically different configurations can you make with a given number of matchsticks on a flat surface? Certain restrictions apply:

1. An edge consists of a single matchstick, and the only point where two matchsticks may touch is at their ends.

2. The matchsticks must lie flat on the surface, but two figures are considered identical if one can be deformed in three-dimensional space without separating the joints (as if the figure were picked up and moved) to resemble the other.

All the possible configurations for one, two and three matchsticks are shown below. How many different configurations can you make with four matchsticks? Five matchsticks?

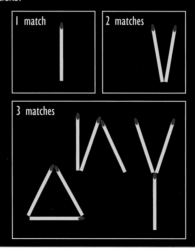

66 **POINTS AND LINES**

91

DIFFICULTY: ●●●●●●●●●●
COMPLETION: ☐ TIME: _____

MATCH POINT

In the figure below, the three matchsticks come together at a point. Can you create a figure out of matchsticks so that both ends of every matchstick are connected with exactly two other matchsticks in this way? Note that the matchsticks may meet only at their ends, and there can be no overlapping. What shape conforms to this rule and yet possesses the fewest number of matchsticks?

92

DIFFICULTY: ●●●●●●●○○○
COMPLETION: ☐ TIME: _____

TOUCHING DAGGERS

Can you arrange these eight daggers so that each one touches at least five others?

WATT'S LINKAGE

Examine the mechanical linkage shown below. The arms are anchored to the mounts on one end but may move freely on the other. And the red link connects the blue arms and constrains their motion. Given that information, can you determine the path of the white point in the middle of the red linkage through a full cycle of motion?

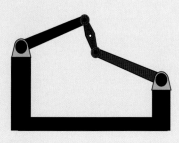

SWING TRIANGLE

In this mechanical linkage, the green arms are anchored to the blue base but both the arms and the red triangle, though linked, are otherwise free to swing back and forth. Can you trace the path of the white dot through one full swing of the linkage?

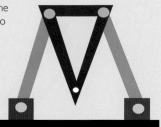

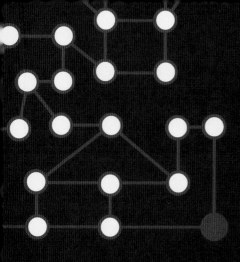

4

Graphs and Networks

Graphs and networks are two-dimensional systems of dots, vertices, or nodes that are connected by lines or edges. In this chapter, you'll search for routes and circuits that will lead you through a variety of graphs and networks. Many of these problems must be solved by trial and error, which is one reason why they make for incredibly challenging and satisfying puzzles.

INTELLIGENT LADYBUG

The ladybug at the bottom of the diagram wants to meet up with her friend at the top. To get there, she'll have to cross the field of colored flowers. Each color represents a different direction—either up, down, left or right. The black squares are deep pits that must be avoided.

Can you figure out the directions represented by each color and find the path the ladybug must take to cross the field?

MYSTERY TRACKS

Can you figure out what could have made these tracks in the sand?

FOUR-POINTS GRAPH

Disregarding rotations and reflections, can you find all the different ways some or all of the four points shown below may be connected using straight lines?

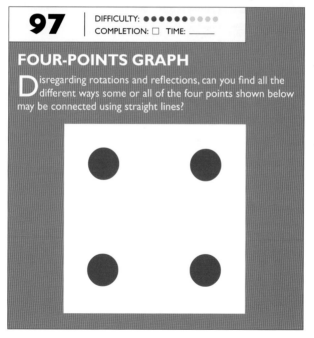

DIFFICULTY: ●●●●●●●●●●
COMPLETION: □ TIME: _____

EULER'S PROBLEM

The object of these puzzles is to trace the complete pattern marked out by the white lines without picking up your pencil or backtracking over any sections. Your lines may cross only at the red points.

Can you do all eleven? If not, which ones do you find impossible to solve?

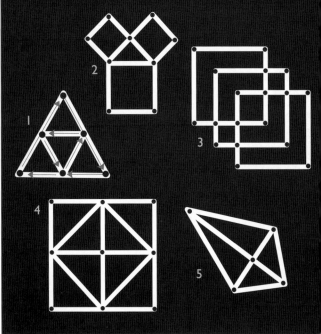

DIFFICULTY: ●●●●●●●●●○○
COMPLETION: ☐ TIME: _____

HAMILTONIAN CIRCUIT

A Hamiltonian circuit is a continuous path that passes once through each point of a graph. Can you find the Hamiltonian circuit for the eleven-point graph illustrated below?

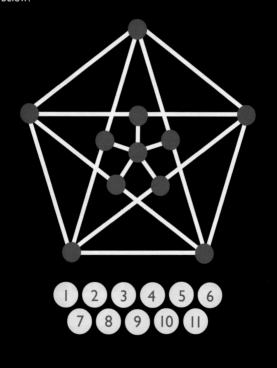

DIFFERENT ROUTES

This puzzle has one rule: Always follow the arrows. Can you find all the allowable routes from "in" to "out" that adhere to the rule?

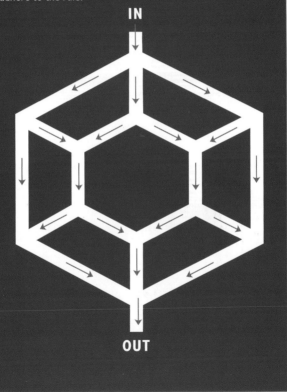

IN

OUT

101

NEIGHBORS

Three neighbors live in a gated compound. Each of their houses is painted a different color, and each has a private gate that is painted to match the house. Ideally, all three houses would be connected to their own gates by paths that didn't cross any of the other paths, but as you can see, there is a problem: the red and green paths intersect.

Can you draw new paths that would make the neighbors happy?

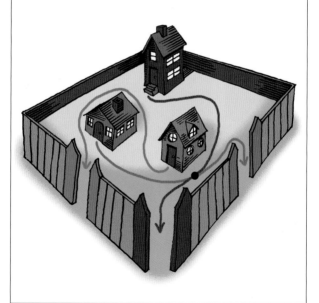

102

DIFFICULTY: ●●●●●●○○○○
COMPLETION: ☐ TIME: _____

TRAVERSING STARS

Can you walk along all the yellow paths outlining the four interconnected stars in one continuous line? You may cross your path and visit each red dot a number of times, but you may not retrace any path.

103

DIFFICULTY: ●●●●●●●○○○
COMPLETION: ☐ TIME: _____

WORM TRIP

A worm crawls only along the edges of a box measuring 2 by 2 by 3 centimeters. What is the longest distance the worm can travel without retracing any of its steps?

104

MARS PUZZLE

There are twenty scientific outposts scattered on the surface of Mars, each marked with a letter and each linked by a canal to at least two other stations. Starting at the outpost marked T and visiting each station just once, follow the various canals to spell out a complete English sentence.

Can you find a solution?

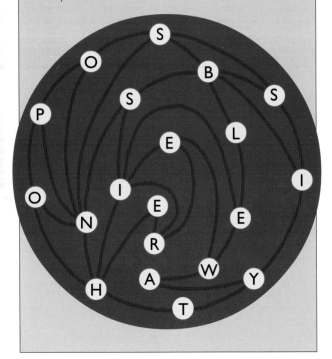

FOUR SCHOOLS

Four children from four different families attend four different schools. Each school is a different color and gives its students notebooks that are the color of the school. Can you lead each student to his or her school without letting any one path cross another?

106

UTILITIES I

The object of this puzzle is to draw lines connecting each animal to all the animals that are different in color without connecting any animals that are the same color. For example, a red fish could be connected to a green fish and a yellow nautilus but not a red clam. Can you draw all the lines connecting the appropriate animals without allowing any of the lines to cross?

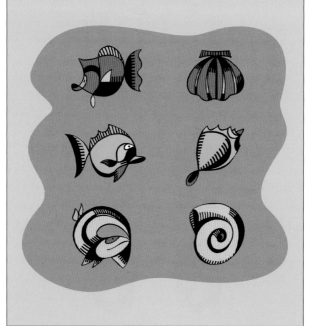

UTILITIES 2

Draw lines connecting each animal to all the animals different in color without connecting any animals that are the same color. How many interconnecting lines can you draw without allowing any of the lines to cross?

UTILITIES 3

Draw lines connecting each animal to all the animals that are different in color without connecting any animals that are the same color. How many interconnecting lines can you draw without allowing any of the lines to cross?

MISSING ARROWS 1

Two arrows are missing from the pattern shown at right. Can you add the missing arrows so that they help create a consistent pattern throughout the grid?

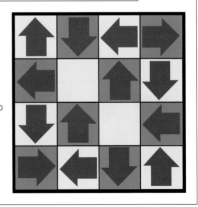

EVEN NUMBER ROUTE

This is another simple route problem with a small twist: the only allowable path from the circle marked "start" to the one marked "finish" involves traveling over an even number of segments. Can you find the shortest allowable path?

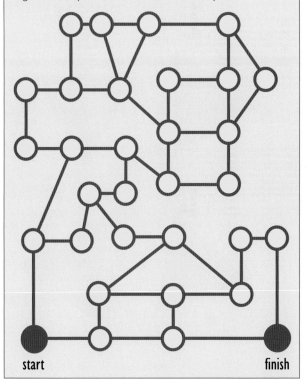

start   finish

LIGHTING THE LAMPS

The three lamps and three batteries shown below are arranged around an empty space for a triangular circuit board.

Using just your eyes and imagination, can you work out which of the three numbered circuit boards can be placed into the empty space so that each lamp will be powered by its own battery?

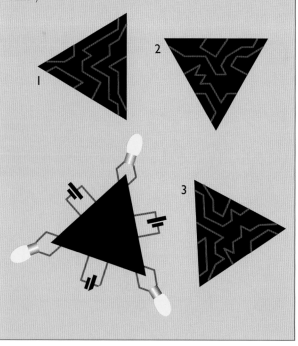

112

PRINTED CIRCUITS 1

Printed circuits are two-dimensional graphs—the junctions carry out electronic operations, while the lines carry electrical signals from place to place. If the lines cross, there will be a short-circuit and the device will fail.

Can you connect the five pairs of colored circuits on this circuit board without crossing any lines? The connecting lines must remain in the white area.

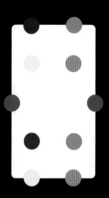

113

PRINTED CIRCUITS 2

Can you draw five lines to connect the five pairs of colored circles? All connecting lines must run along the white lines of the grid, and no connecting lines may intersect.

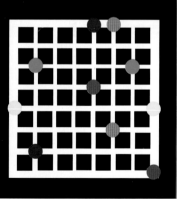

PRINTED CIRCUITS 3

Can you draw eight lines to connect the eight pairs of colored circles? All connecting lines must run along the white lines of the grid, and no connecting lines may intersect.

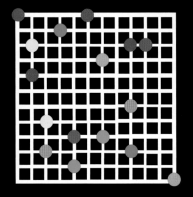

DICE ARROWS

How many different ways can you put six arrows on the faces of a cube?

MINIMAL CROSSINGS

The seven points shown in red are all interconnected by means of twenty-one numbered lines. The lines cross at ten different points. Can you arrange the lines so that there are fewer intersections?

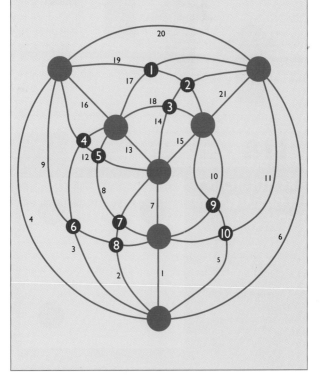

FIVE ARROWS

Rearrange the four arrows to form five arrows.

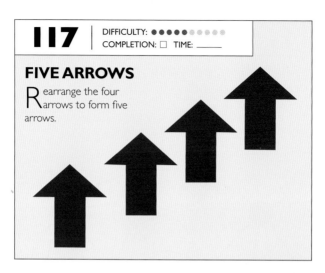

FOUR-POINT TREE GRAPH

Tree graphs are points connected by lines that don't possess closed loops. How many different tree graphs can you find that connect the four points shown at right?

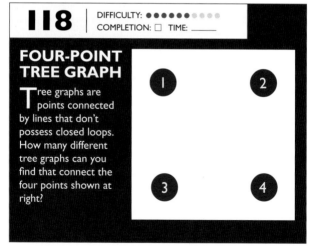

DIFFICULTY: ● ● ● ● ● ○ ○ ○ ○ ○
COMPLETION: ☐ TIME: _____

TREE CHAIN

Nineteen beads lie on a table. Can you join them with string to create a tree graph?

What is the smallest number of branches you can draw between nineteen beads, or nineteen points? Remember that since it is one graph, each point must be linked to every other point by some number of branches. And since it is a tree graph, there can be no closed loops. Is there a general rule for the minimum number of branches needed?

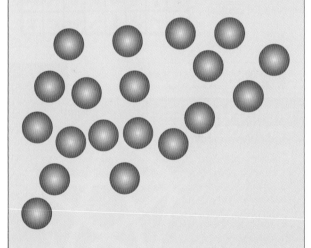

120

MISSING ARROWS 2

Can you work out where the five missing arrows should point?

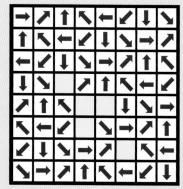

121

DIGRAPH PENTAGON

Each path between two of the numbered points allows travel in just one direction, which is marked with an arrow. With that in mind, can you find the route that will allow travel to all five points?

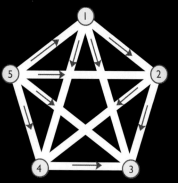

Curves and Circles

A curve is a line that continuously bends but has no angles. Some are open: the line never returns to its starting point. Others join up with themselves to form closed curves, such as the circle and the ellipse. The puzzles in this chapter explore these varied and fascinating forms—and their three-dimensional counterpart, the sphere.

PURSUIT

A horse runs in a straight line; a person runs toward the horse at all times. Can you determine the shape of the path the runner takes in pursuit of the horse?

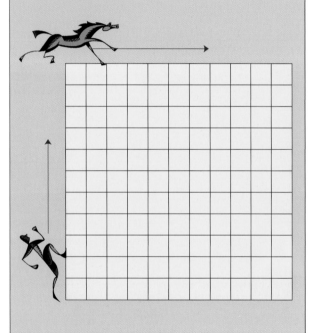

WHY ROUND?

Why are manhole covers round? Can you find three reasons why round is the best possible shape? And the answer "Because manholes are round" doesn't count!

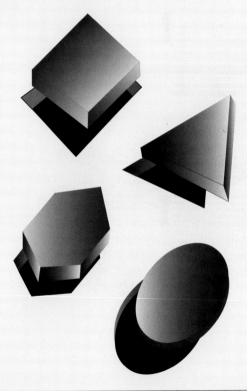

124

DIFFICULTY: ●●●●●●●○○○
COMPLETION: ☐ TIME: _____

ROLLING STONE

People once moved heavy weights by means of rollers made of logs. The circumference of the two identical logs shown here is exactly 1 meter. If the logs roll one whole turn, how far will the weight be carried forward?

DIFFICULTY: ●●●●●●●●○○
COMPLETION: ☐ TIME: _____

CRESCENTS OF HIPPOCRATES

The ancient Greek geometer Hippocrates of Chios discovered this problem while trying to square the circle. He constructed overlapping semicircles on the sides of a right triangle, as shown at right. Can you determine the total area of the two red crescents?

DIFFICULTY: ●●●●●●●○○○
COMPLETION: ☐ TIME: _____

CIRCLE IN THE SQUARE

Which is greater, the sum of the black areas or the sum of the red areas?

SQUARE VASE

Can you divide the red vase and reassemble the parts to form a perfect square? This is possible in two different ways, one that divides the vase into three parts and another that divides it into four parts.

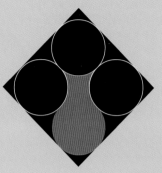

CIRCLE RELATIONSHIP

One circle is circumscribed around a square; another circle is inscribed within the same square. How are the areas of the two circles related?

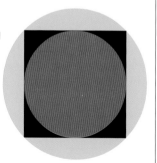

DIFFICULTY: ●●●●●●●●○○○
COMPLETION: ☐ TIME: _____

SICKLE OF ARCHIMEDES

A circle is divided in half along its diameter, and two additional semicircles are constructed along that diameter, as shown here. A line (L) is drawn from the point on the diameter where the two circles meet and extended perpendicularly from the diameter to the circumference of the large semicircle.

The area of the large semicircle that is not covered by the smaller semicircles has the form of a sickle, an ancient tool used for harvesting grain. Can you guess what the area of the sickle might be?

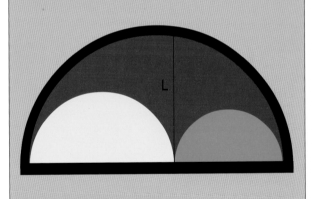

130

DIFFICULTY: ●●●●●●○○○○○
COMPLETION: ☐ TIME: _____

COIN MATTERS

You must rearrange the pyramid of six coins into a hexagon that possesses a hole large enough for a seventh coin. Can you do this in just five moves?

A move consists of sliding a single coin along a flat surface to a new position so that it is in contact with at least two other coins. When moving a coin, you cannot move or jostle any other coin.

131

DIFFICULTY: ●●●●●○○○○○○
COMPLETION: ☐ TIME: _____

UPSIDE-DOWN COINS

The object is to turn the pyramid of ten coins upside down, moving one coin at a time to a new position in which it touches two or more coins.

It is easy to do this in six moves. Can you do it in three?

CIRCLES AND TANGENTS

How many essentially different ways can you find to arrange two circles of unequal size on a plane?

If a tangent is a straight line touching a curve at a single point, and a common tangent is a straight line tangent to two circles, can you find the total number of common tangents to the two circles for all the arrangements of two circles?

Would it make any difference if the circles were the same size?

133

DIFFICULTY: ●●●●●●●○○○
COMPLETION: ☐ TIME: _____

SEVEN CIRCLES PROBLEM

Start with any circle. (Use the red one in the diagram as a reference.) Add six circles around the circumference of the circle so that each of the new circles touches two other new circles and the red circle. Imagine that three of the circles (yellow in the diagram) become larger and larger and the green circles become smaller and smaller, though the green and yellow still remain in contact. Imagine that the yellow circles become so large that they even intersect. What will be the ultimate outcome?

134

DIFFICULTY: ●●●●●●○○○○
COMPLETION: ☐ TIME: _____

POLYGONS IN A CIRCLE

Five points are randomly distributed on the circumference of a circle. From any of those points, a continuous line may be drawn that connects the other points in the polygon before returning to the original point.

How many different polygons can be drawn with these five points?

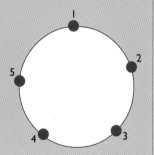

CIRCLES COLORING

The pattern of colored circles on the top contains all the logical clues for filling in the blank circles on the bottom. Size has nothing to do with color, since circles of equal size have different colors.

Can you figure out the pattern, and color in the circles properly?

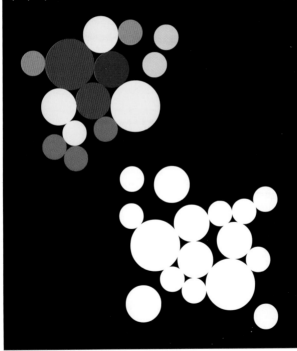

136

DIFFICULTY: ●●●●●●○○○○
COMPLETION: ☐ TIME: _____

ORANGE AND YELLOW BALLS

Can you stack six yellow balls and four orange balls in a triangle so that no three yellow balls form the corners of an equilateral triangle? The example at right is obviously wrong because the three yellow balls do, in fact, form such a triangle.

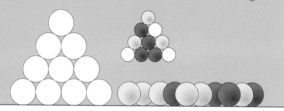

137

DIFFICULTY: ●●●●●●○○○○
COMPLETION: ☐ TIME: _____

JUMPING COINS

You must stack the six numbered coins into two piles of three coins each. But in order to do so, you must move each coin by jumping over exactly three other coins. As an example of an allowable first move, coin 2 can jump over 3, 4 and 5 to stack on coin 6.

Can you stack the coins in five moves or less?

NINE-POINT CIRCLE

The white triangle has some interesting properties: the midpoints of the sides, the bases of the altitudes and the midpoints of the line joining the vertices to the orthocenter (the common intersection of all three altitudes of the triangle) all line up on the circumference of a circle.

Does every triangle form that sort of nine-point circle?

● midpoints of sides
● bases of the altitudes
● midpoints to orthocenter

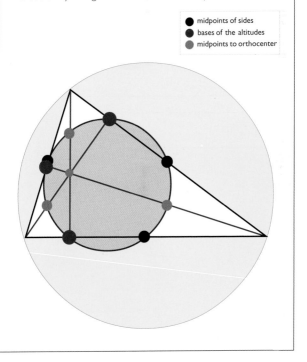

139

TOUCHING CIRCLES

Three circles touch at three points, shown here with black circles. Can you find the minimum number of identical circles in a plane that are required to create nine touching points?

140

INSCRIBED CIRCLES

The large black circle has a diameter of 1 unit. It is inscribed by an equilateral triangle and a square, as shown.

Can you determine the diameters of the three inscribed circles?

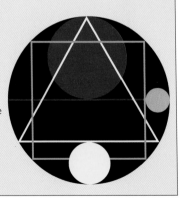

DIFFICULTY: ●●●●●●●●○○○
COMPLETION: □   TIME: _____

TANGENTS TO THE CIRCLE

Three circles of different sizes are distributed randomly, as shown. Pairs of tangents are drawn around the circles, with a surprising result: the three intersection points for the tangents lie along a straight line.

Is this just a coincidence, or will it always happen?

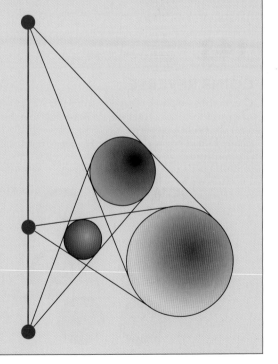

142

DIFFICULTY: ●●●●●●○○○○
COMPLETION: ☐ TIME: _____

INDIANA ESCAPE

Jones is running down a square tunnel, desperately trying to avoid being crushed by a giant round stone that is rolling toward him. The width of the tunnel is just about the same as the diameter of the sphere; both are 20 meters.

The end of the tunnel is too far for Jones to reach in time. Is he doomed?

143

DIFFICULTY: ●●●●●○○○○○
COMPLETION: ☐ TIME: _____

COINS REVERSE

Seven coins are placed heads up in a circle. You would like them all to be tails up, but you are allowed to move them only if you turn five over at a time. Can you follow that rule repeatedly to eventually wind up with all seven coins tails up? How many moves will it take?

ROLLING COIN

The yellow coin rolls over seven immovable coins in the configuration shown below. By the time the yellow coin returns to its starting position, how many complete revolutions will it have made? And which direction will the coin be facing?

145

ROLLING CIRCLE: HYPOCYCLOID

A smaller circle rolls inside a fixed circle twice its diameter. What path will the red point trace as the small circle completes one circuit?

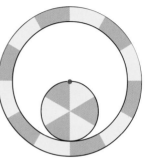

146

NORTH POLE TRIP

An airplane leaves the North Pole and flies due south for 50 kilometers. Then it turns and flies east for another 100 kilometers.

At the end of that journey, how far is the plane from the North Pole?

147

DIFFICULTY: ●●●●●●●○○○
COMPLETION: ☐ TIME: _____

SPHERE VOLUME

A cylinder, a sphere and a cone are identical in height and width. Do their volumes have any sort of special relationship?

148

DIFFICULTY: ●●●●●●○○○○
COMPLETION: ☐ TIME: _____

LOOPED EARTH

Imagine the Earth as a perfect sphere. (It is not, but picture it this way for the sake of this puzzle.) Then imagine the equator is a long belt that has been looped around the Earth and fastened snugly.

If you loosened that belt by 2 meters and pulled the belt away from the surface, how much slack would there be? In other words, how high could you pull the belt? The answer is either .03 meters, .33 meters or 3.3 meters—but which?

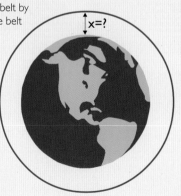

x=?

QUICKEST DESCENT

Four identical balls on four different tracks are released simultaneously. Which of the tracks—bent, straight, circular or cycloidal—will deliver its ball to the end of the slope the fastest?

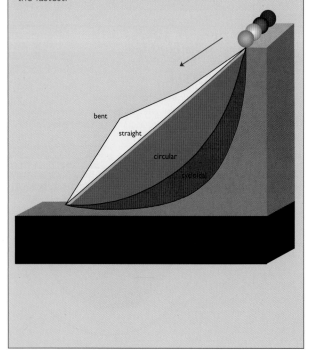

150

DIFFICULTY: ●●●●●●●○○○
COMPLETION: ☐ TIME: _____

CUTTING A SPHERE

Imagine that this sphere has been divided with four straight cuts, all of which go right through the sphere. Can you determine the maximum number of pieces into which the sphere has been divided?

151

DIFFICULTY: ●●●●●●●○○○
COMPLETION: ☐ TIME: _____

HELIX

A rope winds around a large cylindrical pipe, making four complete turns, as shown. The circumference of the pipe is 4 meters and its length is 12 meters. Can you figure out how long the rope is?

CYCLOID AREA

$\mathbf{C}$an you find the area under the cycloid? How does the length of the curve relate to the size of the circle that generates the line?

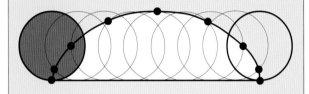

SPHERE SURFACE AREA

$\mathbf{A}$ sphere fits exactly inside a thin-walled cylinder that has a height and diameter equal to the diameter of the sphere. Which object has more surface area, the sphere or the cylinder?

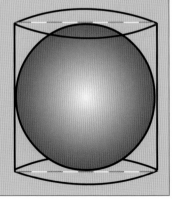

154

DIFFICULTY: ●●●●●●○○○○
COMPLETION: ☐ TIME: _____

CONICS

In his book *Conics*, dated 225 B.C., the Greek scholar Apollonius revealed that a cone with a circular base can be cut to form a family of curved shapes. For the cuts marked 1 through 4 in the illustration, which curved shapes will result?

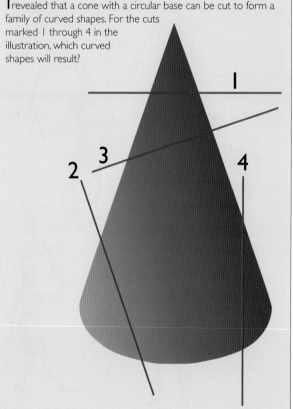

SWORDS AND SCABBARDS

As they prepare for battle, four warriors draw their swords from their scabbards. One sword is completely straight. Another is a semicircle. A third sword has the form of a wavy curve. And the fourth has the three-dimensional form of a helicoid spiral, as shown. Something isn't right about this story. What is it?

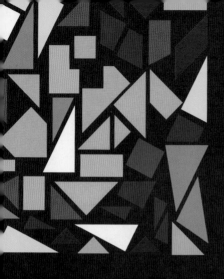

Shapes and Polygons

S hapes may seem quite simple, consider a common circle or square, but they are, actually, very mathematically complex objects. Polygons—closed figures bordered by straight lines—are particularly fascinating. This chapter will challenge you to find ways in which shapes and polygons can be put together and broken apart.

ODD SHAPE

One of these seven shapes shown is not like the others.
Which shape? And why?

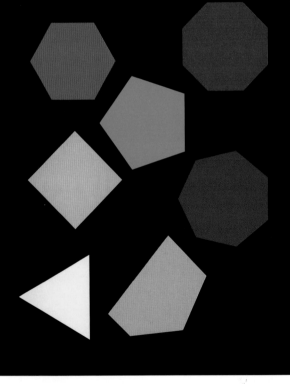

157

DIFFICULTY: ●●●○○○○○○○
COMPLETION: ☐ TIME: _____

ODD ONE OUT

Which of these shapes is different from the other four?

158

DIFFICULTY: ●●●●●●●○○○
COMPLETION: ☐ TIME: _____

EULER'S FORMULA

Examine the complex polygonal map illustrated below. Then count the number of points represented by the black dots. From that number, subtract the number of sides, and add to that result the number of regions.

What is the number? Will it be the same for every polygon, regardless of its size, shape and complexity?

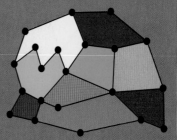

CONVEX-CONCAVE

There's a number missing from the middle of the red polygon. What should it be?

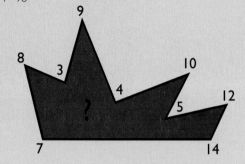

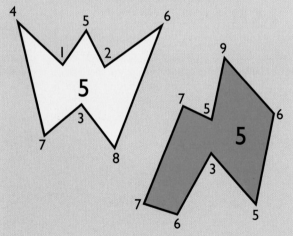

160

PEG-BOARD AREA

The Peg-Board shown at right has a rubber band stretched around the four red pegs. Can you calculate the area enclosed by the rubber band without measuring anything?

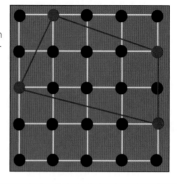

161

HEXAGON IN-OUT

A regular hexagon circumscribes a circle, which circumscribes another regular hexagon. The inner hexagon has an area of 3 square units. What is the area of the outer hexagon?

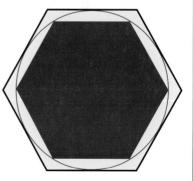

CONVEX QUADRILATERAL

Begin with five randomly placed points on a plane. Will it always be possible to connect four of those points to create a convex quadrilateral?

TRIANGLE COUNT

A mask of unknown shape has been placed over this collection of triangles. Based on what you can see, how many triangles were there to begin with?

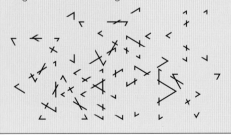

OVERLAPPING TRIANGLES

Eight smaller equilateral triangles in three sizes (with sides of 1, 2 or 3 units) partly overlap a larger triangle with sides 5 units long. Can you tell which is greater, the red area of the big triangle or the blue area of the small triangles?

HIDDEN TRIANGLE

Trisect the angles of a triangle, as shown. Note that three points within the triangle form an equilateral triangle.

Does such an equilateral triangle appear in every trisected triangle?

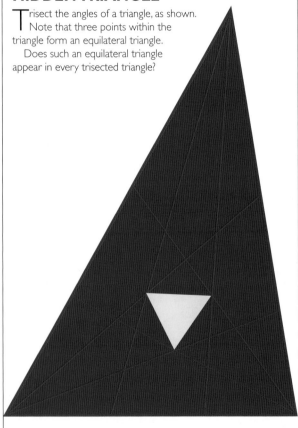

HOW MANY TRIANGLES?

How many triangles of different sizes can you find in this pattern?

TRIANGLES IN QUADRILATERALS

A straight line divides this quadrilateral into two triangles. Can you find a quadrilateral (which is simply a polygon with four sides) that can be divided with a straight line into three triangles?

HEXAPATTERNS

All but one of the smaller patterns are composed of the same twenty-four colored pieces that make up the large hexagon.

Which hexagon is the odd one out?

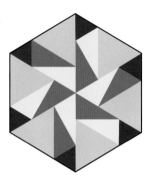

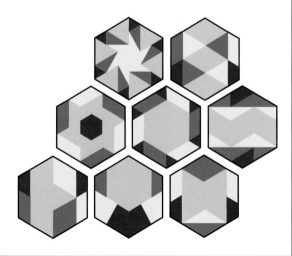

169

DIFFICULTY: ●●●●●●●●●○
COMPLETION: ☐ TIME: _____

HINGED SCREEN

A hinged screen made of two identical panels is placed in the corner of a room, as shown. At what angle should the panels be opened to enclose—with the walls—the largest possible area?

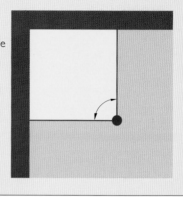

170

DIFFICULTY: ●●●●○○○○○○
COMPLETION: ☐ TIME: _____

POLYGON AREAS

These two regular polygons—a regular hexagon and an equilateral triangle—have equal perimeters. What is the ratio of their areas?

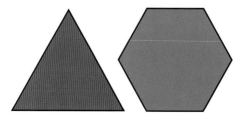

171

TRIANGLES INSCRIBED 1

How many triangles can you draw from the vertices of a heptagon that don't possess sides that are also sides of the heptagon?

In a square and a pentagon, for instance, you can't draw such a triangle; in a regular hexagon you can draw two, as shown.

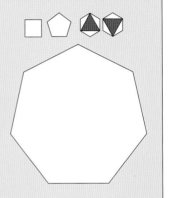

172

TRIANGLES INSCRIBED 2

How many triangles can you draw from the vertices of an octagon that don't possess sides that are also sides of the octagon?

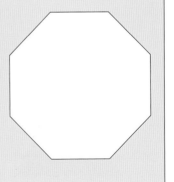

HOW MANY CUBES?

Can you find six three-dimensional cubes portrayed in perspective in the pattern below?

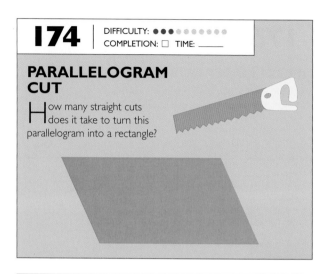

174

DIFFICULTY: ●●●○○○○○○○
COMPLETION: ☐ TIME: _____

PARALLELOGRAM CUT

How many straight cuts does it take to turn this parallelogram into a rectangle?

175

DIFFICULTY: ●●●●○○○○○○
COMPLETION: ☐ TIME: _____

TRIANGULATION

How many diagonals are needed to divide a heptagon, a nonagon and an undecagon into triangles? How many triangles will result from the divisions?

PEG-BOARD TRIANGLES

Not counting rotationally symmetrical variations and translations, there are exactly eleven different triangles that can be formed by connecting three points on a three-by-three Peg-Board. Ten are shown here. Can you find the eleventh?

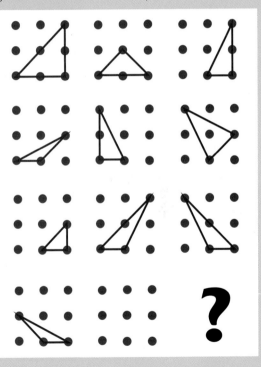

ART GALLERY

An art gallery has fourteen walls of identical length. Several revolving security cameras keep a watch on the walls. The gallery owner would like to redesign the space so that the total number and length of walls stay the same and yet every square inch of wall can be watched with just one revolving camera. What design accomplishes this goal?

JAPANESE TEMPLE PROBLEM FROM 1844

Five squares are arranged as shown. Can you demonstrate that the area of the green square is equal to that of the green triangle?

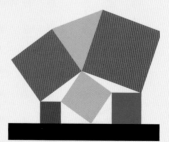

TRISECTING TRIANGLE

A line connects each vertex of this triangle to a trisection point on the opposite side. (Such lines are called cevians, for Giovanni Ceva, an Italian mathematician who lived from 1648 to 1734.) The three lines divide the triangle into seven regions, with the area of each region a multiple of $1/21$ of the total area.

Can you work out the proportional area of all seven regions?

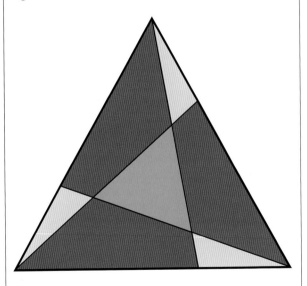

180

DIFFICULTY: ●●●●●●●○○○
COMPLETION: ☐ TIME: _____

CONDITION TRIANGLE

Four sets of strips of different lengths are shown. The sets are of lengths 3, 4 and 6; 3, 5 and 7; 4, 5 and 9; and 3, 5 and 9. Are there any sets of strips that cannot form a triangle when joined together?

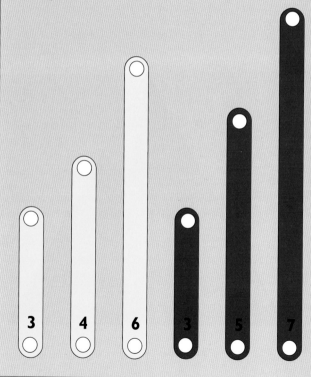

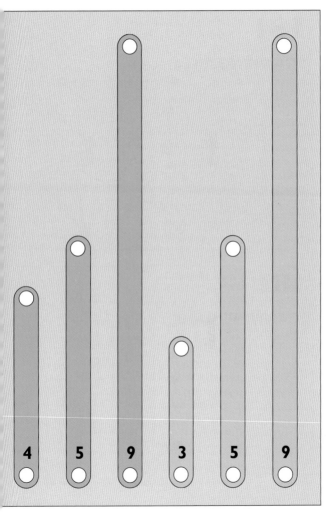

181

SCANNING ART

In a strangely shaped modern art gallery, every square inch of floor space can be watched by the six revolving security cameras (red dots) mounted in the corners. Can you find the minimum number of cameras needed to do the same job? Where must they be placed?

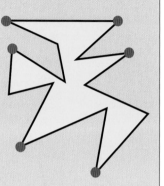

182

SCANNING BANK

Five revolving security cameras (red dots) are installed in the corners of a bank. The cameras can cover every square inch of floor area. Where would you mount just three cameras so that they can cover the same area?

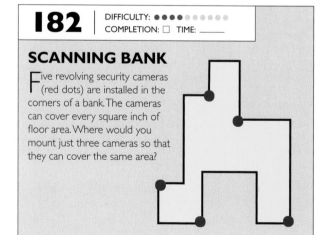

NAPOLEON'S THEOREM

Draw a triangle as shown here in blue. Construct an equilateral triangle on each of its faces. Then, from the center of those new triangles, form another equilateral triangle.

Will this work every time? What if the triangles are constricted inward?

This theorem has been attributed to Napoleon, an enthusiastic amateur mathematician.

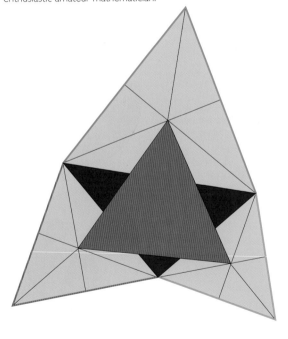

184

DIFFICULTY: ●●●●●●●●○○○
COMPLETION: ☐ TIME: _____

SHARING CAKES

At a birthday party three cakes are cut as shown and divided between two groups. One group gets the red pieces, while the other gets the yellow.

Cake 1 is cut through the center three times, making six 60° angles.

Cake 2 is also cut three times, but through an off-center point. Again, the cuts make six 60° angles.

Cake 3 is cut through the same off-center point, but now four times, making eight 45° angles.

Did each group get identical shares of the three cakes?

cake 1

cake 2

cake 3

PICK-UP POLYGONS

Ten regular polygons lie in a heap. Each polygon can be picked up, but only when no other figure lies on top of it Can you tell in what order the polygons may be removed?

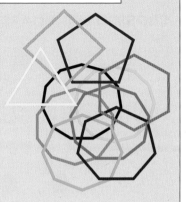

INVISIBLE SQUARE

A square has disappeared except for four points, which lie in the exact positions they occupied on the four sides of the square. Can you re-create the position of the square?

CROSSED PEG-BOARD

Peg-Boards are found in many games and educational activities. Almost all of them consist of a matrix of holes arranged in squares and squares-within-squares. On the board shown here, the pegs or holes are represented as dots.

Other boards may be arranged differently—say, in triangular matrices—but the same principles will apply.

How many squares of any size can you create by connecting four pegs on the board shown? Hint: The squares do not need to have horizontal bases.

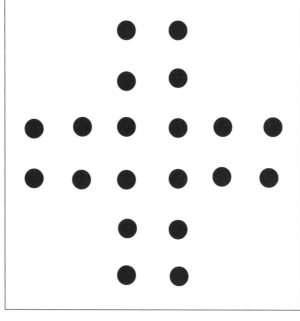

7

Patterns

Patterns are found in a fantastic variety of places in the natural world. They indicate an underlying system of order which is very pleasing to the human mind. From permutations and factorials to ordered arrangements and magic squares, in this chapter you'll be challenged to detect existing patterns and generate new patterns all your own.

FACTORIALS

How many different words can you make from the letters *O*, *N* and *W*, using each one only once?

BOYS AND GIRLS

Elementary schoolchildren on a field trip sit in groups of four, so that every girl sits next to at least one other girl. How many permutations are possible?

MAGIC CUBE 1

The three-by-three cube shown below can be divided into twenty-seven one-by-one cubes. Can you fill each of the smaller cubes with one of three colors (red, green or yellow) in such a way that each vertical column and each horizontal row contains all three colors? Each color will appear exactly nine times.

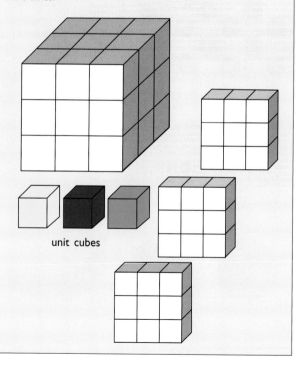

unit cubes

MAGIC STAR I

Can you place the numbers from 1 to 10 on the blank circles so that the sum along any straight line equals 30?

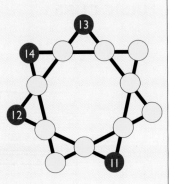

PERMUTATIONS

Line up the three fruits in as many different arrangements as possible. How many did you find?

193

COLOR PAIRS

Sixteen pairs of circles are shown below. Using just yellow, red, green and blue, can you fill up each pair with a different combination of colors?

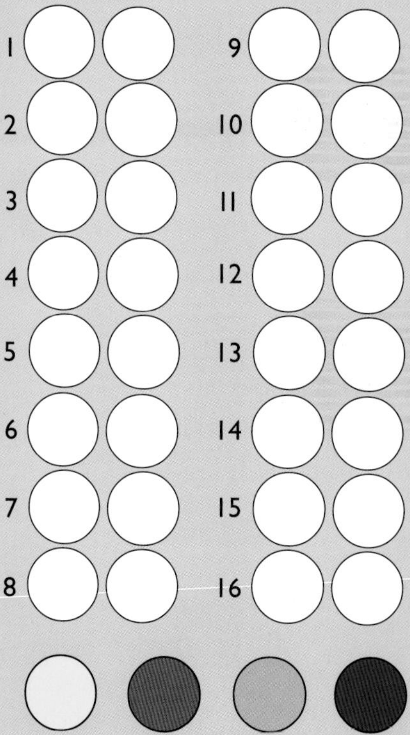

1 ◯◯   9 ◯◯

2 ◯◯   10 ◯◯

3 ◯◯   11 ◯◯

4 ◯◯   12 ◯◯

5 ◯◯   13 ◯◯

6 ◯◯   14 ◯◯

7 ◯◯   15 ◯◯

8 ◯◯   16 ◯◯

SEATING PROBLEM

In how many different ways (ignoring rotations) can eight family members seat themselves around an octagonal dinner table?

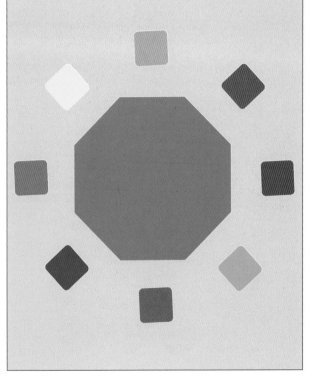

MAGIC PENTAGRAM

Can you place the numbers 1 to 12 (except for 7 and 11) on the circles so that the sum of the numbers on any straight line equals 24? The numbers 3, 6 and 9 have been placed to guide you.

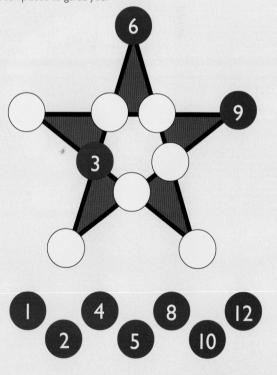

COLOR NECKLACE

With red, yellow, green and blue beads, can you design a necklace in which the sixteen possible color pairs occur only once in each direction?

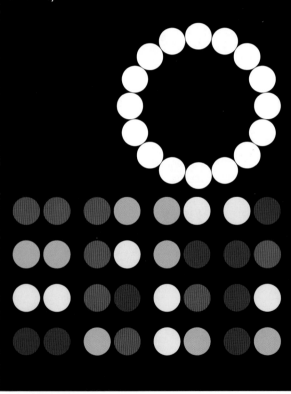

197

DIFFICULTY: ●●●●●●○○○○
COMPLETION: ☐ TIME: _____

MAGIC SQUARE 1

Can you distribute the numbers 1 through 9 in such a way that when the central number in any horizontal, vertical or diagonal line of three is subtracted from the outer two, the sum is always the same?

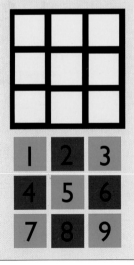

198

DIFFICULTY: ●●●●●●○○○○
COMPLETION: ☐ TIME: _____

MAGIC SQUARE 2

Can you distribute the numbers 1, 2, 3, 4, 6, 9, 12, 18 and 36 in such a way that when multiplied, each horizontal, vertical and diagonal line has the same result?

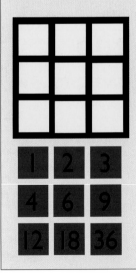

199

MAGIC SQUARE 3

Can you distribute the numbers 1, 2, 3, 4, 6, 9, 12, 18 and 36 in such a way that when the central number of any horizontal, vertical or diagonal line is divided into the product of the outer two numbers of the line, the result is always the same?

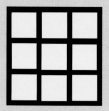

200

MAGIC SQUARE 4

Fill in the squares with the numbers 1 through 12 so that no two consecutive numbers appear either vertically, horizontally or diagonally.

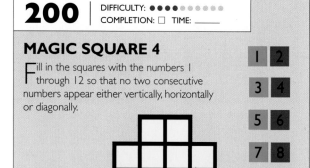

201

MAGIC SQUARE OF DÜRER

The German artist Albrecht Dürer engraved this magic square of order 4 in his 1514 etching *Melancholia*. It is one of many magic squares that is magic in more ways than the simple definition requires.

First, can you fill in the missing numbers (see inset) so that the sum of every horizontal, vertical and main diagonal line totals 34?

Then can you find other ways in which this square is magic?

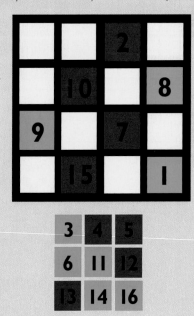

202

MAGIC SQUARE 5

Some of the squares of the grid for this five-by-five magic square are highlighted. Can you distribute the numbers 1 through 25 so that the sum of every horizontal, vertical and main diagonal line is equal—and only odd numbers appear in the highlighted squares?

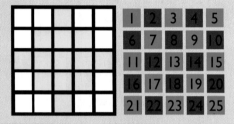

203

MATHEMAGIC

Can you place the numbers from 1 to 8 in the circles so that no adjacent numbers are connected by the black lines?

The inset shows an example of a puzzle that doesn't work.

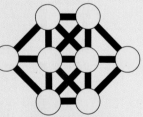

MAGIC SQUARE 6

Can you distribute the numbers 1 through 8 and −1 through −8 so that the sum of every horizontal, vertical and main diagonal line equals zero?

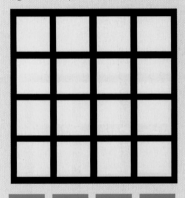

THE LO-SHU

According to Chinese legend, the Lo-Shu dates back to at least the fifth century B.C. It is the oldest and simplest magic square.

The object of the Lo-Shu is to arrange the tiles numbered from 1 to 9 in the cells of the board so that the sum of every row, column and diagonal is the same. Not counting reflections and rotations, there is one answer.

Can you determine the sum without even solving the puzzle?

HINGED MAGIC SQUARE

Flipping the numbered tiles along their hinges covers some numbers and reveals others that were hidden. The back of each tile has the same number as the front; behind the tile is a number that is twice as big as the original.

Can you flip just three numbered tiles so that the sum of every vertical, horizontal and main diagonal line equals the magic constant of 34?

MONKEYS AND DONKEYS

Five monkeys and three donkeys live in a zoo. If you had to select one monkey and one donkey, how many different combinations could you choose from?

MAGIC CIRCLES I

At each point of intersection for the four circles is a spot for a number.

Can you add the numbers shown below to the empty spots so that the set of numbers along each circle adds up to 39?

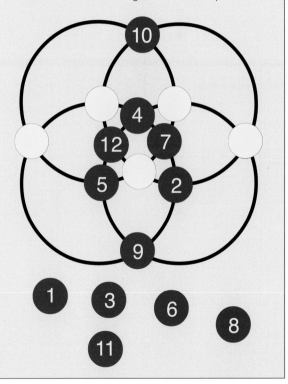

SQUARE NUMBERS SQUARE

Can you place four different numbers in the circles here so that the sum of the two numbers along any given side is a square of another number?

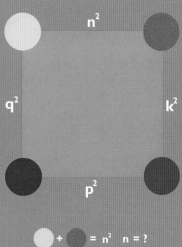

MAGIC HEXAGON I

Can you add the missing numbers to the seven blank circles so that the sum of the numbers along any straight line is 21?

SQUARENUMBER TRIANGLE

Can you place three different numbers in the circles at right so that the sum of the two numbers along any given side is equal to the square of another number?

●+○ = n^2 n=?
●+● = k^2 k=?
●+○ = p^2 p=?

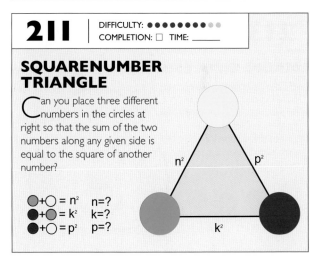

212

MAGIC CIRCLE 2

Can you distribute the numbers from 1 to 9 so that every line across the wheel adds up to 15?

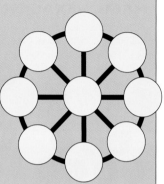

213

MAGIC CIRCLES 3

Can you distribute the numbers from 1 to 6 on the intersections of the three circles so that the sum of the numbers on each circle is identical to the other two?

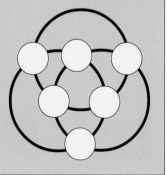

HEPTAGON MAGIC

Can you arrange the numbers from 1 to 14 along the sides of a heptagon in such a way that the three numbers on each side add up to 26?

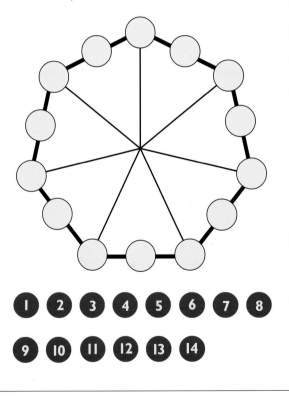

MAGIC CUBE 2

Can you distribute the numbers from 1 to 12 on the edges of the cube in such a way that the sum of the four edges on each face equals 26?

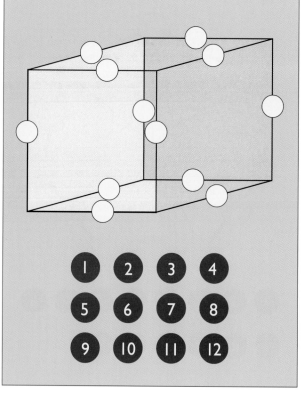

MAGIC CIRCLES 4

Arrange the numbers from 1 to 18 so that the sum of any two symmetrical pairs of numbers is 19. Three pairs have already been placed. Can you place the rest?

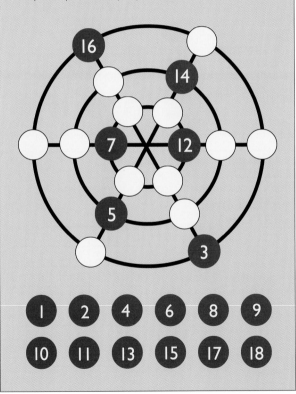

MAGIC STAR 2

Can you add the missing numbers to the nine blank circles so that the sum of the numbers along any straight line equals 26?

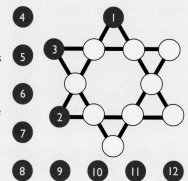

GRIDS AND ARROWS

The yellow squares around the square grid must be filled with one arrow each, drawn so that the arrow points vertically, horizontally or diagonally along the grid. Can you fill in the arrows in such a way that the number of arrows pointing to each square in the grid equals the number shown in that square?

	↓	↙				
	3	2	1	2	2	↙
↗	2	1	3	1	4	
	2	4	2	5	2	
	4	2	5	2	3	
→	3	4	2	3	3	
	↗	↑				

219

MAGIC HEXAGON 2

Volumes have been written about magic squares, but the "magic" can be embodied by other polygons, such as triangles, circles and hexagons. For example, can you distribute the numbers from 1 to 19 in the hexagonal game board illustrated below so that the sum of every straight line is identical? Can you work out what the magic constant must be?

To keep the puzzle from being too difficult, we've seeded some of the hexagons with numbers. You need to place only the remaining numbers.

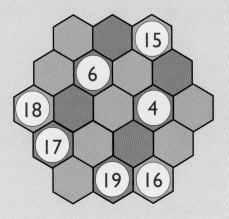

220 DIFFICULTY: ●●●●●●●○○○
COMPLETION: ☐ TIME: _____

SQUARE DANCE

Each row is a sequence of predictable motions for five black squares, with one pattern missing from each sequence. By studying the three patterns given in each row, can you complete all four sequences?

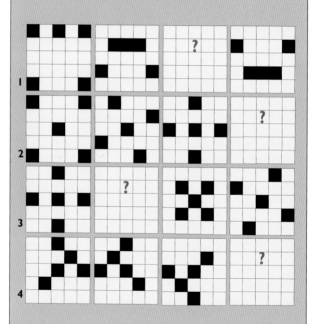

TWO FRUITS IN THREE BOWLS

How many different ways can you serve two pieces of fruit with three bowls?

ROWS OF COLOR

Using only red or blue, color the points of intersection one by one. Can you fill in the whole pattern without allowing any single line to have four points of the same color?

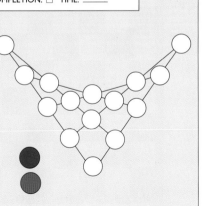

TROMINOES AND MONOMINO

Can you cover a full chessboard with the twenty-one trominoes (dominoes made up of three squares) and one monomino shown here?

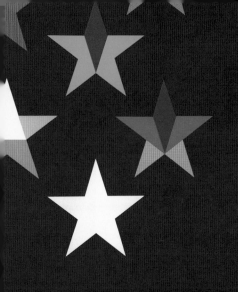

8

Dissections

One of the best ways to learn about shapes is to cut them apart and reassemble the pieces to form new shapes. There are many ways to divide a given shape, and some of those divisions—called dissections—are particularly complex. Dissections are found in lots of games, and this chapter will highlight some of the best and most satisfying dissection conundrums.

224

DIFFICULTY: ●●●●●○○○○○
COMPLETION: ☐ TIME: _____

LUCKY CUTS

Can you dissect this horseshoe into six pieces with only two straight cuts?

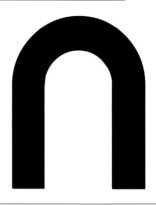

225

DIFFICULTY: ●●●●○○○○○○
COMPLETION: ☐ TIME: _____

MIRROR FLIPS

Each of the multicolored pieces can be flipped around the red mirror lines. Using only your visual imagination, can you work out what shape is produced when all four pieces are flipped?

226

SEPARATING MONKEYS

Each of the four monkeys needs an identical compartment that is fenced off from the other monkeys. Following the grid lines on the six-by-six square, can you find two possible ways of separating the monkeys?

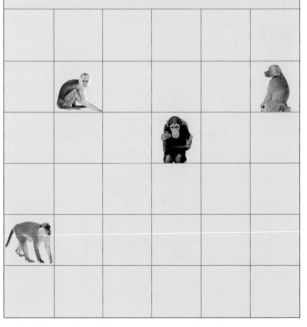

DIFFICULTY: ●●●●○○○○○○○○
COMPLETION: ☐ TIME: _____

FENCES

Can you erect fences along the grid lines so that each of the four types of animals has a pen that is identical in size and shape?

228

QUARTERING SQUARE

A five-by-five square with a unit square missing from the center can be cut along the grid lines into four congruent parts. (Removing the center square allows each quarter to have an area of six square units.) There are seven ways to accomplish this; one solution is shown. Can you find the other six?

229

HALVING SHAPE 1

Can you divide this irregular shape into two congruent parts? Then can you dissect the shape again to make four congruent parts? There are two possible quartering solutions, one of which does not follow the grid lines.

HALVING SHAPE 2

Can you dissect this irregular shape into two congruent parts?

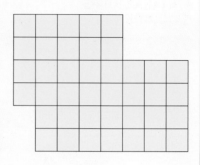

HALVING SHAPE 3

Can you divide this shape into two congruent parts?

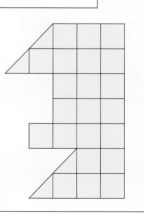

232

HALVING SHAPE 4

Can you divide this shape into two congruent parts?

233

QUARTERING SHAPE 1

Can you help Simon divide his L-shaped carpet into four congruent parts?

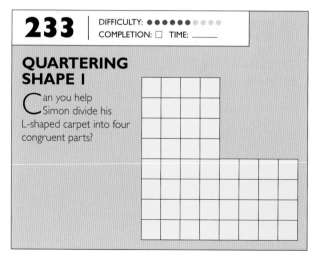

234

DIFFICULTY: ●●●●●●●○○○
COMPLETION: □ TIME: _____

QUARTERING SHAPE 2

Can you divide this shape into four congruent parts?

235

DIFFICULTY: ●●●●●●●●○○○
COMPLETION: □ TIME: _____

QUARTERING SHAPE 3

Anna must divide this trapezoidal shape into four congruent parts. Can you show her how to do it?

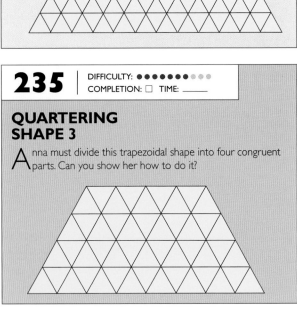

CONNECTED SHAPES I

This nonconvex polygon is divided into twenty-four identical triangles, each of which is filled in with one of four colors. Can you rearrange the triangles within the boundary of the polygon to make four identical connected shapes? Each of the shapes should be of one color, and the shapes can be counted as identical even if they are reflections or rotations of one another.

237

CONNECTED SHAPES 2

Some shapes comprise two sections connected by a single point. Can you divide this polygon into two identical connected shapes?

238

LADYBUG SEPARATION

When ladybugs are hungry, they begin to fight. Can you place three straight fences in such a way that each ladybug is separated into its own compartment?

GREEK CROSS INTO SQUARES

Can you dissect this Greek cross into nine pieces that can fit together to form either five small squares or one large one?

FLIES

As you can see in the diagram, every one of the nine flies on the grid has its row, column and diagonal to itself. Can you move three of the flies just one space each—horizontally, vertically or diagonally—and still preserve their right to an exclusive row, column and diagonal?

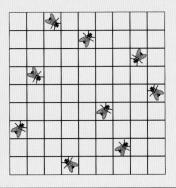

SQUARE INTO TWO SQUARES

Can you dissect the five-by-five square into the fewest number of pieces needed to make both a four-by-four square and a three-by-three square?

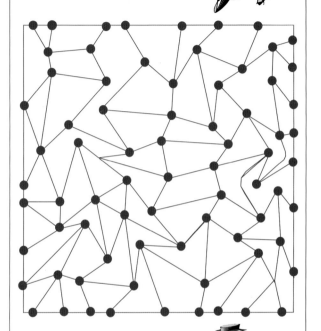

SUBMARINE NET

Navy frogmen must cut a path through the enemy net to allow the submarine to pass through, but they have only enough time to cut through the ropes of the net; the knots are too thick.

Can you find the path from the top to the bottom that will require the fewest cuts?

243

DIFFICULTY: ●●●●●●●●○○○
COMPLETION: ☐ TIME: _____

SQUARE INTO THREE SQUARES

Can you dissect this seven-by-seven square into the fewest pieces necessary to form three smaller squares: a six-by-six, a three-by-three and a two-by-two?

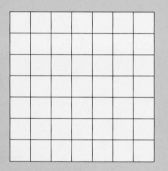

244

DIFFICULTY: ●●●●●●●○○○
COMPLETION: ☐ TIME: _____

HINGED TRIANGLE

This equilateral triangle has been dissected into four parts. Hinges, marked in red, connect the parts to each other. If you leave the blue piece fixed and swing the others around their hinges, you can rearrange the pieces to form a new shape. Can you work out what that new shape must be?

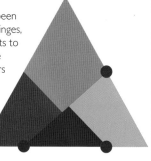

245

DIFFICULTY: ●●●●●○○○○○
COMPLETION: ☐ TIME: _____

TRIANGLE FITTING

How many of the small figures can you place in the larger one without overlap?

TRIANGLE TO STAR

This equilateral triangle is composed of twenty-four identical right triangles. Just by looking at it, can you work out how to rearrange the pieces to form a perfect six-pointed star?

247 | DIFFICULTY: ●●●●●●●●●●○○○ COMPLETION: ☐ TIME: _____

IMPERFECT TRIANGLE

Using the triangular grid as a guide, divide this equilateral triangle with sides 11 units long into smaller-integer triangles. What is the smallest number of such triangles that will completely cover the figure?

248 | DIFFICULTY: ●●●●●●●○○○○○ COMPLETION: ☐ TIME: _____

GUNPORT PROBLEM 1

Many interesting problems have been built around blocks whose sides, like dominoes, possess a 2:1 ratio. One such puzzle is the gunport problem, in which one must find a way to construct the most one-by-one holes with two-by-one blocks. Can you arrange ten two-by-one blocks on a four-by-seven grid to make eight holes, each of which is one-by-one?

249

GUNPORT PROBLEM 2

Can you arrange eleven dominoes on the four-by-eight board to make ten holes?

250

GUNPORT PROBLEM 3

Can you arrange fourteen dominoes on a five-by-eight board to make twelve holes?

GUNPORT PROBLEM 4

Can you arrange twenty-seven dominoes on an eight-by-ten board to make twenty-six holes?

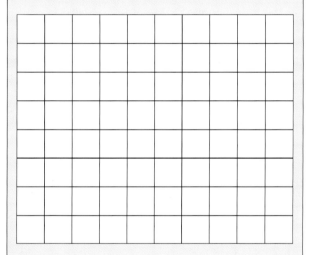

IMPERFECT SQUARE SPLIT

Fifteen squares can form an imperfect thirteen-by-thirteen square, as shown on the right. If you remove one of the five-by-five squares, can you reassemble the remaining squares to form a twelve-by-twelve imperfect square (meaning it's divided into smaller squares, two or more of which are the same size)?

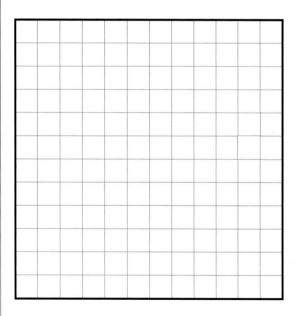

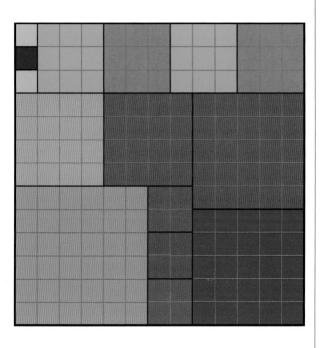

UNCOVERED SQUARE

If you try to fit the five chevron shapes onto the four-by-four board, one square will always be uncovered. After all, the five chevrons each cover an area of three units, and the board has an area of sixteen units. But can that uncovered square be anywhere on the board?

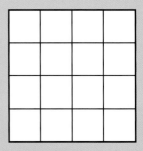

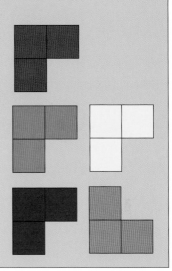

RECTANGLES IN TRIANGLE

Four examples of right isosceles triangles partially filled with squares or rectangles are shown. Just by looking at them, can you tell in which examples the shapes cover the greatest proportion of the triangle?

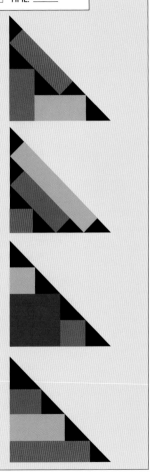

255 | DIFFICULTY: ●●●●○○○○○○
COMPLETION: ☐ TIME: _____

REPLI-POLYGON

Can you work out how many of the smaller four-square T-tiles it takes to completely fill its larger replica? How would they fit?

256 | DIFFICULTY: ●●●●●○○○○○
COMPLETION: ☐ TIME: _____

REGULAR TESSELLATIONS

A regular tessellation is a mosaic made up of identical regular polygons that completely fill a plane. There is an infinite number of regular polygons—from the equilateral triangle and the square up to the circle, which may be considered a regular polygon with an infinite number of sides. Can you work out how many of those regular polygons are capable of tessellating a plane?

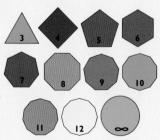

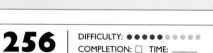

POLYOMINOES

Illustrated below are the nine different ways to join up to four identical squares so that their sides meet perfectly.

Can you find all the different ways to join the sides of five identical squares?

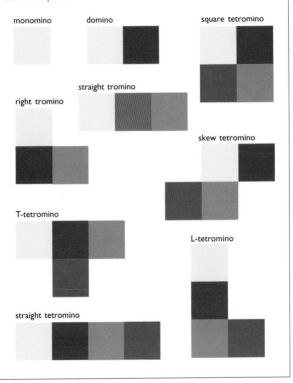

monomino

domino

square tetromino

straight tromino

right tromino

skew tetromino

T-tetromino

L-tetromino

straight tetromino

BATTLESHIPS

In the classic game of battleship, a ten-by-ten grid is covered with a fleet of ten ships: four submarines (each a unit square), three destroyers (two squares each), two cruisers (three squares each) and a battleship (four squares). The ships must be placed on the grid in such a way that no two ships touch—not even at corners.

Can you arrange the nine smaller ships in such a way that it is impossible to place the battleship anywhere on the board?

9

Numbers

Numbers are symbols and like the objects they represent, they can be put together to form patterns. The simplest pattern, a sequence, is just a list of numbers in a certain order; a more advanced pattern, called a series, is the sum of the numbers in a sequence. Recognizing these—and others—often presents quite a difficult challenge. This chapter will push you to develop a deeper understanding of the logic and fun of numbers.

HEX NUMBERS

The first four hexagonal numbers are illustrated here. The series runs 1, 7, 19 and 37. By examining the differences between successive hexagonal numbers, can you work out what the next hexagonal number must be?

I

7

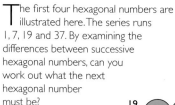

19

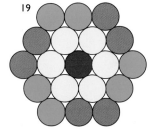

37

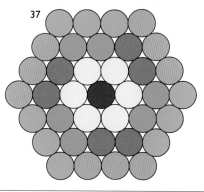

260

SQUARE NUMBERS

A number that is multiplied by itself is called a square. The first six square numbers are illustrated in figurate form. Can you continue the sequence by examining the difference in value between successive squares? What is the seventh square?

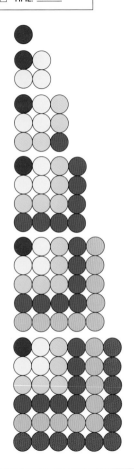

261

DIFFICULTY: ●●●●●●●●○○○
COMPLETION: ☐ TIME: _____

THREE-DIMENSIONAL FIGURATE NUMBERS

There are three-dimensional analogues to the plane figurate numbers. Such numbers can be found by packing spheres in three-dimensional pyramids: three-sided pyramids give tetrahedral numbers; four-sided pyramids give square pyramidal numbers.

The first three tetrahedral numbers are 1, 4, 10.

The first three square pyramidal numbers are 1, 5, 14.

Examine the differences in both series.

Can you continue them both?

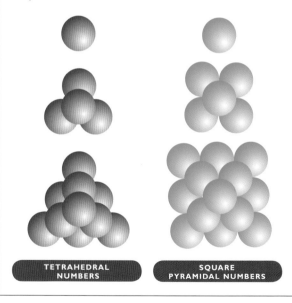

TETRAHEDRAL
NUMBERS

SQUARE
PYRAMIDAL NUMBERS

262

LAGRANGE'S THEOREM

A famous theory of numbers states that every whole number can be expressed as the sum of, at most, four squares. This can be demonstrated graphically: Examine these two rectangles, one with 12 square units and one with 15 square units. Can you show how those rectangles are each composed of four smaller squares?

12

15

263

COUNTING GAUSS

When Carl Friedrich Gauss was six years old (back in 1783), his schoolteacher asked the students to add up all the numbers from 1 to 100.

Unfortunately for the teacher, who was hoping to keep the class occupied, it took young Gauss only a few seconds to work out the answer. He had spotted a pattern in the sequence and could provide the answer via a simple operation that he performed in his head. Of course, with a mind like that, it didn't take very long for Gauss to become one of Germany's most celebrated mathematicians and scientists.

Can you figure out what Gauss did to come up with the answer?

APPLE PICKERS

If five apple pickers can pick five apples in five seconds, how many apple pickers would it take to pick sixty apples a minute?

STACKING ORDER

You are asked to stack these eight blocks according to four simple rules:

1. Just one block must lie between the two red blocks.
2. Two blocks must lie between the pair of blue blocks.
3. Three blocks must separate the pair of green blocks.
4. Four blocks must separate the pair of yellow blocks.

Can you figure out how to do it?

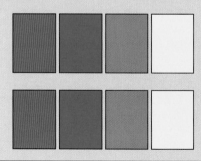

PAGE NUMBERS

You pull out a page from a newspaper and find that pages 8 and 21 are on the same sheet. From that, can you tell how many pages the newspaper has?

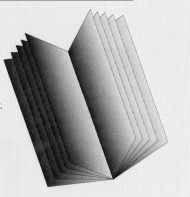

SUM SQUARES

The first nine digits are arranged in a square, as shown, so that the number formed on the first line can be added to the number on the second line to make the number on the third line. Can you make another square that adds up in that way?

$$
\begin{array}{cccc}
 & 2 & 1 & 8 \\
+ & 4 & 3 & 9 \\
\hline
= & 6 & 5 & 7 \\
\end{array}
$$

268

DIFFICULTY: ●●●●●●○○○○○
COMPLETION: ☐ TIME: _____

LADYBUG SPOTS

My daughter raises ladybugs. Her collection includes eight with red spots and one without any spots. If 55 percent of her ladybugs have yellow spots, what's the smallest possible size of her collection?

269

DIFFICULTY: ●●●●●○○○○○○
COMPLETION: ☐ TIME: _____

EIGHT CARDS

Can you make the two columns of numbers add up to the same total by moving just two cards around?

270

DIFFICULTY: ●●●●●●●●●●●●

COMPLETION: ☐ TIME: _____

NUMBER CARDS 1

Can you fill in the three blanks on each of the four cards with numbers from 1 to 6 so that any given pair of cards has exactly one number in common?

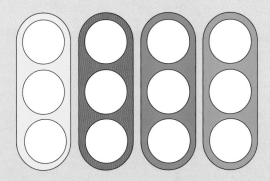

NUMBER CARDS 2

Can you fill in each of the four blanks on all five cards with a number from 1 to 10 in such a way that every number appears only twice and every pair of cards has exactly one number in common?

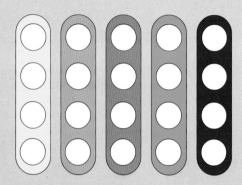

DIFFICULTY: ●●●●●●○○○○○○
COMPLETION: □ TIME: _____

NUMBER CARDS 3

Can you fill in each of the spaces on the six cards with a number from 1 to 15 in such a way that each number appears only twice and every pair of cards has exactly one number in common?

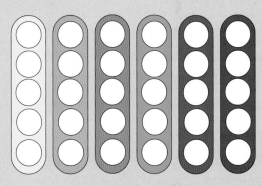

273

TEN-DIGIT NUMBERS

How many different ten-digit numbers can be written with the digits 0 to 9?
(Starting a number with 0 is not allowed.)

1,234,567,890

274

NUMBER MATRIX

Examine the matrix. Can you fill in the missing number?

I	I	I	I
I	3	5	7
I	5	13	25
I	7	25	?

ARITHMAGIC SQUARE

Can you fill in the blanks with the numbers from 1 to 9 so that each mathematical equation is correct? (The operations read from left to right and from top to bottom.)

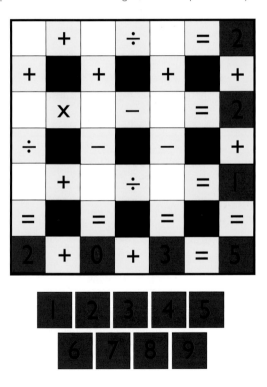

DIFFICULTY: ●●●●●○○○○○
COMPLETION: ☐ TIME: _____

DIVISION

What is the smallest number divisible by 1, 2, 3, 4, 5, 6, 7, 8 and 9?

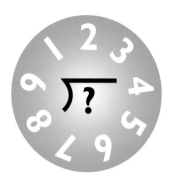

DIFFICULTY: ●●●●●●●○○○
COMPLETION: ☐ TIME: _____

BIRTHDAY CANDLES

On every birthday since I was born, I have had a cake decorated with the appropriate number of candles. I have blown out 210 candles so far. How old am I?

278

FIBONACCI SEQUENCE

This series is the beginning of the famous Fibonacci number sequence. Discovered by the Italian mathematician Leonardo Fibonacci in the thirteenth century, the sequence appears throughout nature. The organic growth patterns in daisies, sunflowers and nautilus shells follow spirals described by the sequence.

Examine the sequence at right. Can you fill in the next number?

279

NUMBER SEQUENCE I

Examine the series of numbers. Can you work out the logic behind it and fill in the next number in the sequence?

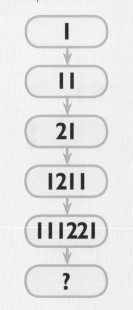

280

HONEYCOMB COUNT

What are the four missing numbers in the honeycomb?

281

NUMBER SEQUENCE 2

Can you uncover the logic behind this sequence and fill in the next number in the series?

282

PERSISTENCE SEQUENCE

Examine the sequence. Can you discover the underlying logic and fill in the final number?

77 ► 49 ► 36 ► 18 ► ?

283

AGE DIFFERENCE

I have a friend who became a professional magician more than 45 years ago, shortly after the birth of his son. He told me recently that his age and the age of his son are numerically reversed. If he is 27 years older than his son, how old are they?

284

TIME WISE

A very clever digital clock had a programming error and displayed the pattern shown below when the actual time was 9:50. Can you move the minus sign to a position where it can help display the correct time?

285

MISSING NUMBERS

The nine empty boxes must be filled with the digits from 1 to 9. Can you work out the way to place the numbers so that the mathematical operations are correct?

WINE DIVISION

There are fourteen wineglasses on a table: seven are full, seven are half full. Without changing the amount of wine in any glass, can you divide the glasses into three groups so that each has the same total amount of wine?

JIGSAW

A jigsaw puzzle has 100 pieces. A move involves joining two clusters of pieces, or joining one piece to a cluster. Work out the fewest moves needed to complete the puzzle.

288

DIFFICULTY: ●●●○○○○○○○
COMPLETION: ☐ TIME: _____

ADD A NUMBER

Can you work out what number can be added to both 170 and 30 so that the resultant sums have a ratio of 3:1?

$$170 \quad\quad 30$$
$$\underline{+X} \quad\quad \underline{+X}$$
$$Y \quad\quad\quad Z$$

$$\frac{Y}{Z} = \frac{3}{1} \quad X = ?$$

289

DIFFICULTY: ●●●●●●○○○○
COMPLETION: ☐ TIME: _____

RIGHT EQUATION

Can you move one digit to a new position so that the equation below is correct? (Moving signs is not allowed.)

62−63 = 1

MONASTERY PROBLEM

Place digits from 0 to 9 in the outer squares of the grid. Every red square must contain the same number; every yellow square should contain the same number; the sum of the numbers on each side should equal nine. How many different solutions can you find, not counting the one shown?

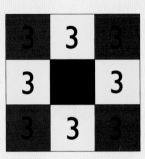

FLOWERS PURPLE AND RED

There are exactly forty flowers, red and purple, in a garden. And no matter which two flowers you pick, at least one will be purple. Can you work out how many red flowers there are?

FLOWERS PURPLE, RED AND YELLOW

There are purple, red and yellow flowers in a garden. Anytime you pick three flowers, at least one will be red and at least one will be purple. From that information, can you work out how many flowers there are?

COUNTING ANIMALS

I went to the zoo and saw the camels and the emus. If, all told, I saw thirty-five heads and ninety-four feet, how many camels and emus did I see?

294

ZOO MIX

On another trip to the zoo, I counted thirty-six heads and one hundred feet. Can you work out how many birds and how many beasts I saw?

295

THREE'S COMPANY

There are nine people in your circle of friends, and you want to invite them to dinner, three at a time, over the next twelve Saturdays. Is there a way to arrange the invitations in such a way that pairs of friends meet each other at your dinners just once?

Kate
David
Lucy
Emily
Jane
Theo
Mary
James
John

296

CAT LIVES

The following is derived from an ancient Egyptian puzzle.

A mother cat has spent seven of her nine lives. Some of her kittens have spent six, and some have spent only four.

Together, the mother and her kittens have a total of twenty-five lives left.

Can you tell with certainty how many kittens there are?

297

JAILHOUSE WALK

Nine prisoners are handcuffed in groups of three for their daily exercise. If the warden wants to arrange the men so that no two individuals are chained side by side more than once over the course of a six-day period, how might he handcuff them?

HINGED RULER I

Five unmarked rulers have been hinged at two points, as shown. What lengths should each of the rulers have so that one or a combination of rulers can measure every distance from 1 to 15 units?

MINIMAL LENGTH RULER

Four marks have been placed on the ruler at the top so that you can use it to measure every whole number of distance units from 1 to 6. Can you place five marks on the lower ruler so that you can measure the ten possible whole distances between 1 and 11 units? The two end marks have been made, so you need place only the middle three.

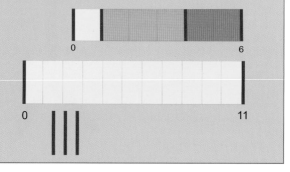

300

LADYBUG FAMILY

One-fifth of the ladybug family flew to the garden with the yellow roses. One-third of the family flew to the violets, and three times the difference between these two numbers flew to the red poppies far away. And the mother of the ladybug family went to the river to do laundry. When all the ladybugs met up back home, how many were there?

301

HINGED RULER 2

Three unmarked rulers are hinged at one point, as shown. What three lengths should the rulers have so that, singly or in combination, they can measure every length from 1 to 8 units?

It can't be done? Try including measurements in which the rulers are folded back against one another.

302

DIFFICULTY: ●●●●●●○○○○

COMPLETION: ☐ TIME: _____

PROGRESSION I

Examine this beautiful geometric progression. Can you work out the total area of the red triangles as a proportion of the area of the outer square?

303

DIFFICULTY: ●●●●●●●○○○

COMPLETION: ☐ TIME: _____

PROGRESSION 2

What is the area of the red arm as a proportion of the entire square?

304

GOLYGONS

The mathematician Lee Sallows of the University of Nijmegen in The Netherlands conceived of the following problem.

Start at the yellow point on the grid. Pick a direction and "walk" one block. At the end of the block, turn left or right and walk two more blocks; turn left or right and then walk three blocks. Continue this way, walking one more block in each segment than before. If after a number of turns you return to the starting point, then the path you have traced is the boundary of a golygon.

The simplest golygon has eight sides, meaning it can be traced in eight segments. Can you find it?

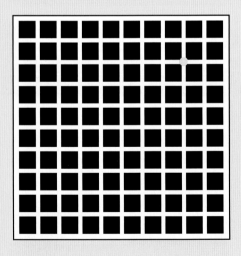

305 | DIFFICULTY: ●●●●●●●●●○○
COMPLETION: ☐ TIME: _____

PRIME DOUBLES

Can you always find a prime number somewhere between any number and its double (excluding 1, of course)?

306 | DIFFICULTY: ●●●●●●●○○○
COMPLETION: ☐ TIME: _____

PRIME CHECK

There are exactly 9!, or 362,880, different nine-digit numbers in which all the digits from 1 to 9 appear. The number below is an obvious example. Of those 362,880 numbers, can you work out how many will be prime—divisible only by 1 and themselves?

123,456,789

307

DIFFICULTY: ●●●●●●●○○○
COMPLETION: ☐ TIME: _____

INFINITY AND LIMIT

Each picture is half the height of the image it is set in. If this pattern continued, there would be an infinite number of pictures. Rather than setting them one inside another, imagine stacking them atop each other. How tall would the tower of pictures grow?

308

AMICABLE NUMBERS

Is it possible for numbers to be not just perfect but friendly or amicable? Examine the numbers 220 and 284. Can you work out the hidden relationship between them?

309

FACTORING

Natural numbers can be either composite or prime. Prime numbers are like the bricks from which composite numbers are made. Indeed, any natural number can be uniquely represented as a product of prime numbers.

Can you find the prime numbers that are the factors of 420?

420

310

DIFFICULTY: ●●●●●●●●●●●
COMPLETION: ☐ TIME: _____

CIRCLE OF DANCE

Anne and her friends are dancing in a circle. The circle is set up so that every dancer is next to two people who are both of the same gender.

How many girls are there if there are twelve boys in the circle?

311

DIFFICULTY: ●●●●●●●●●●●
COMPLETION: ☐ TIME: _____

ADD AND MULTIPLY

What three numbers have a sum equal to their product?

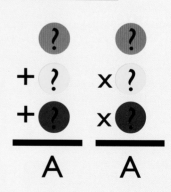

312

HIGHLY COMPOSITE

Composite numbers are the product of two or more primes, but a "highly composite" number has more divisors than any number below it. For example, 12 is a highly composite number, since no number less than 12 has six distinct divisors. Twelve is composed of 1, 2, 3, 4, 6 and 12.

What is the next highly composite number? The answer, of course, has eight divisors.

$$1,2,3,\overline{4,6,12)}12$$

313

HIDDEN MAGIC COIN

One of the most beautiful coin tricks is often explained as a feat of extrasensory perception. But it is really an example of the mathematical concept of parity.

Ask someone to toss a handful of coins on a table. After a quick peek at the result, turn your back and ask the person to turn over pairs of coins at random—as many pairs as he or she likes. Then ask the person to cover up one coin.

When you turn around, you can tell immediately whether the covered coin is showing heads or tails.

Can you work out the mathematical secret at the heart of this trick?

314

DIFFICULTY: ●●●●●●○○○○○
COMPLETION: ☐ TIME: _____

BINARY ABACUS

0

1

Because at heart computers are simply a collection of electronic switches, the base 2—or binary— system of numbers is the language of the information age. Even though binary notation uses just 1s and 0s, it can represent any whole number.

The abacus illustrated here can represent numbers in binary form. Can you work out how you would use it to express 53? What about 63?

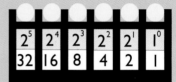

2^5	2^4	2^3	2^2	2^1	1^0
32	16	8	4	2	1

315

DIFFICULTY: ●●●●●●○○○○○
COMPLETION: ☐ TIME: _____

POLICE CHASE

In this game the policeman (the green dot) chases the thief (the red dot). They alternate moves, going from circle to adjacent circle. The policeman catches the thief if, in his move, he can place his green dot on the red dot. Can the policeman catch the thief in fewer than ten moves?

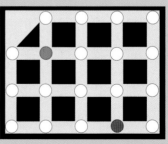

316

HEXABITS

If you divide a hexagon into six wedge-shaped pieces and fill in each section with one of two colors, you can get up to fourteen unique patterns.

Thirteen patterns are shown. Can you work out which one is missing?

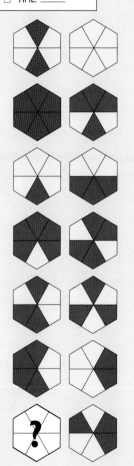

HEXABITS 2

If you divide a hexagon with lines drawn between its vertices, you can fill in the alternating regions with two different colors, as shown. Discounting rotations but accepting reflections as different, there are nineteen unique patterns that can be created in this manner. You have been given seventeen—can you find the other two?

318

DIFFICULTY: ●●●●●○○○○○
COMPLETION: ☐ TIME: _____

THREE GLASSES TRICK

Place three glasses on a table, as shown above. Your goal is to bring all three glasses to the upright position in exactly three moves, turning over two glasses at a time. A quick examination will reveal that this is easy to do—in fact, it can be done after any number of moves.

Once you succeed, turn all three glasses over to the inverted position, as shown below. Then challenge your friends to duplicate your feat.

319

DIFFICULTY: ●●●●●○○○○○
COMPLETION: ☐ TIME: _____

POKER CHIPS PATTERN

Sixteen chips lie on a table in an alternating pattern, as shown.

If you are allowed to slide only two chips into new positions, can you find a way to turn the pattern into horizontal rows of solid colors?

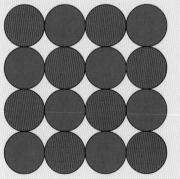

320

DIFFICULTY: ●●●●●●●●○○○
COMPLETION: □ TIME: _____

LAMP IN THE ATTIC

One of the three switches on the ground floor turns on the lamp in the attic. Your job is to find out which of the three switches activates the lamp, but you are allowed only one trip to the attic to check on the light.

Can you figure out how to tell which light switch works?

321

DIFFICULTY: ●●●●●●●●○○○
COMPLETION: □ TIME: _____

RANDOM SWITCHING

There are three unmarked light switches that have been randomly set to "on" and "off" positions. Each is connected to a lamp in another room, which will shine only when all three are in the "on" position.

If you were offered the chance to bet, for even money, that you could turn on the lamp with the flip of just one switch, should you take it?

NECKLACE

Can you work out how many different necklaces can be made using five identical red beads and two identical green ones?

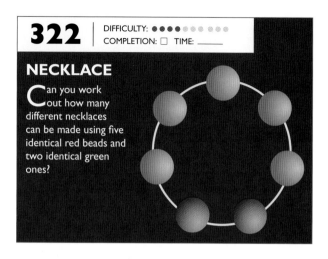

SIX GLASSES PROBLEM

Place six glasses on a table, as shown. Take any pair and invert them. If you continue to invert pairs for as long as you like, will you ever end up with all six glasses upright?
How about all six glasses upside-down?

NECKLACE COLORING

Each necklace has six beads—some red, the rest yellow. From studying the twelve necklaces shown, can you work out the pattern for the thirteenth?

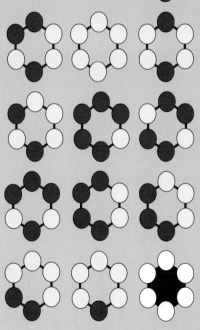

325

DIFFICULTY: ●●●●●●●●○○
COMPLETION: ☐ TIME: _____

BINARY OR MEMORY WHEEL 1

All the possible triplets of digits 1 and 0 can be embodied in three switches, which may be in either the "on" or "off" position. These triplets represent the first eight numbers (including 0) of the binary numbering system. It is interesting to note that, altogether, twenty-four switches are needed to express the first eight digits simultaneously, as shown at right.

In the "binary" or "memory" wheel, the same amount of information can be condensed to just eight switches. To show how, examine the necklace outline. Can you find a way to use four red and four green beads in such a way that all eight triplets will be represented by consecutive beads as you go around the necklace clockwise? Although the beads in the triplet must be consecutive, each triplet need not be next to the other.

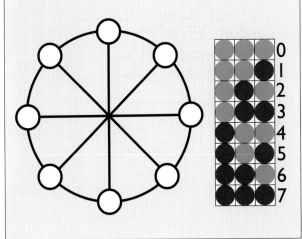

326

DIFFICULTY: ●●●●●●●●●○○○

COMPLETION: ☐ TIME: _____

BINARY OR MEMORY WHEEL 2

Can you make a necklace from eight red beads and eight green beads so that all the four-bead color sequences (embodying the first sixteen binary numbers, including 0) are represented by consecutive beads as you move clockwise around the necklace?

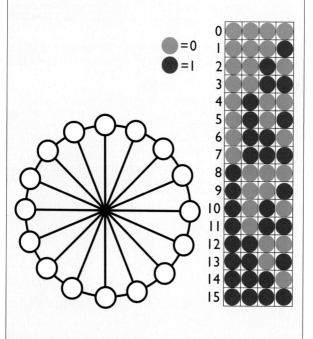

= 0

= 1

Logic and Probability

Probability is the likelihood that an event will occur. It can be measured with values that fall between 0 (which means the outcome is impossible) and 1 (there is absolute certainty). Most events follow the laws of probability, and if we know those laws, our chances of finding the most likely answers are greatly enhanced. These puzzles will challenge you to determine probabilities and use logic to solve seemingly impossible questions.

HIERARCHY

In logic the basic form of reasoning is deduction, in which a specific conclusion is reached based on one or more premises. The conclusion must be true if all the premises are true.

Here is a classic deduction problem that will show you how this works.

In a certain company the positions of chairman, director and secretary are held by Gerry, Anita and Rose—but not necessarily in that order. The secretary, who is an only child, earns the least. And Rose, who is married to Gerry's brother, earns more than the director.

From that information, can you work out who does what?

GIRL-GIRL

Mr. and Mrs. Smith have two children, and they tell you that at least one of them is a girl. Assuming that boys and girls are equally likely, what is the probability that their other child is a girl?

329

FACING SOUTH

How can you build a house that has a window in all four walls but every window faces south?

330

LOGIC SEQUENCE

The lower row of shapes, which is hidden, is in a different sequence than the top row. The hidden row does, however, conform to the following rules:

- Neither the cross nor the circle is next to the hexagon.
- Neither the cross nor the circle is next to the triangle.
- Neither the circle nor the hexagon is next to the square.
- The triangle is just to the right of the square.

Can you work out the hidden sequence?

PARROT

Madame M. decided to buy a parrot to keep her company. But she wanted one that talked. "Does this parrot speak?" Madame M. asked the pet store clerk.

The clerk was unequivocal. "This parrot," he said, "repeats every word he hears."

That convinced Madame M. to buy the bird. But after months of trying to teach the parrot to speak, she never heard a word out of him.

Was the clerk lying? Or is there a piece of important information he left out?

GHOTI

GHOTI

The word in red may seem odd, but it is pronounced just like a common English word. Pronounce the *gh* as in "tough," the *o* as in "women" and the *ti* as in "emotion."

What, then, is the common word that "ghoti" sounds like?

SETTLING THE ACCOUNT

A man ordered dinner at an expensive restaurant. When the meal was brought to him, he looked at it, wrote the note below for the waiter and left the restaurant. The waiter took the note to the cashier, who understood its meaning and placed it in the cash register.

Can you work out what the note meant?

334

COLOR DIE

The same die is shown in four different positions. From this information, can you work out the color of the bottom (or opposite) face of the bottom die?

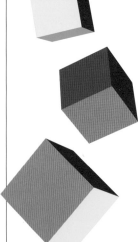

335

WATCHING BIRDS

A great number of birds sit randomly spaced on a wire, each watching its nearest neighbor. Not counting the two birds on the end of the wire, what percentage of the birds sits unwatched?

336

DIFFICULTY: ●●●○○○○○○○
COMPLETION: ☐ TIME: _____

MARRIAGE

Many years ago a man married the sister of his widow. How did he do it?

337

DIFFICULTY: ●●●○○○○○○○
COMPLETION: ☐ TIME: _____

TRUTH TELLERS

Our three children are either liars or truth tellers. Can you determine with certainty how many of each there are?

I am a truth teller.

He says he is a truth teller.

He is not a truth teller–he is a liar!

DRAWING COLORED BALLS

A container holds twenty red balls and thirty blue balls. If you draw a ball without looking, what is the probability that it is a red ball?

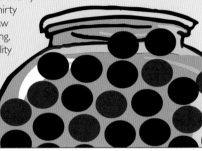

FIGHTING CHANCE

You participate in a virtual reality game in which you are given the chance to fight either one brontosaurus or three smaller stegosaurs in a row.

You know in advance that your chances of defeating the brontosaurus are one in seven, while the probability of defeating one of the stegosaurs is ½.

Which alternative should you choose?

HATCHECK

Six men check their hats at the theater. An inattentive attendant mixes up the claim checks, so when the men return after the show, the hats are essentially handed out at random.

If someone offered you even money to bet that at least one of the men got his own hat back, would you take the bet? In other words, do you believe the probability of one of the six men getting his own hat back is greater than 0.5?

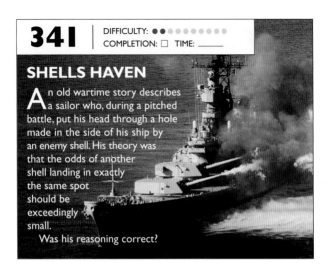

341

DIFFICULTY: ●● ● ● ● ● ● ● ● ●
COMPLETION: ☐ TIME: _____

SHELLS HAVEN

An old wartime story describes a sailor who, during a pitched battle, put his head through a hole made in the side of his ship by an enemy shell. His theory was that the odds of another shell landing in exactly the same spot should be exceedingly small.

Was his reasoning correct?

342

DIFFICULTY: ●●●●●●●● ● ●
COMPLETION: ☐ TIME: _____

THREE COINS PARADOX

Suppose you have three coins—one with a head and a tail, one with two heads and one with two tails—that are dropped in a hat. If you draw one coin from the hat and lay it flat on a table without looking at it, what are the chances that the hidden side is the same as the visible side?

LIKES AND DISLIKES

The picture below shows members of a group I belong to discussing their favorite food. Can you work out who is who and who likes what?

ROULETTE

What is the only sure way to win at roulette?

WORD SQUARE

Word squares are matrices in which the same set of words appears both horizontally and vertically.

Can you fit in the extra letters to form a four-by-four word square?

346

DIFFICULTY: ●●●●●●●●●●●●
COMPLETION: ☐ TIME: _____

HORSE RACE

The will of an eccentric old man stipulated that his two heirs were to stage a horse race and the owner of the losing horse would receive the entire inheritance. At the appointed hour, the race took place, but both heirs kept their horses from crossing the finish line. To break the stalemate, the executor of the will thought up a slight change to the race. Following the executor's idea, the two heirs raced again, and the one who finished first won the inheritance.

How could that be the case if everyone stayed true to the letter of the will?

347

DIFFICULTY: ●●●●●●●●●●●●
COMPLETION: ☐ TIME: _____

DICE STACK

Can you add all the numbers on the unseen sides of the six dice?

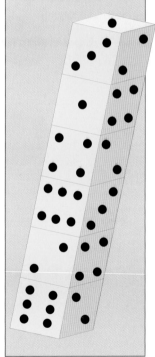

348

DIFFICULTY: ●●●●●●○○○○
COMPLETION: ☐ TIME: _____

ROLLING MARBLES

Peter and Paul are equally good at marbles. If Peter has two marbles and Paul has one, can you work out the probability of Peter winning? To win, a marble must land closest to a fixed point.

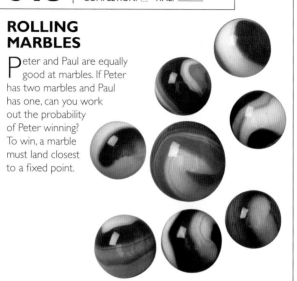

349

DIFFICULTY: ●●●●○○○○○○
COMPLETION: ☐ TIME: _____

REBUSES

Can you solve the two rebus word problems illustrated below?

ME JUST YOU
TIMING TIM ING

350 | DIFFICULTY: ●●●●●○○○○○
COMPLETION: ☐ TIME: _____

THREE MISTAKES

There are three mistakes in the message below.
Can you spot them all?

What are the tree mistake
in this sentence?

351 | DIFFICULTY: ●●●●●●○○○○
COMPLETION: ☐ TIME: _____

COUNTING

There is a secret word hidden in this matrix of letters.
Can you discover it?

R	V	E	O	V	C
S	I	O	V	R	D
V	E	R	C	V	O
R	O	V	E	S	E
E	R	S	C	R	I
C	E	R	E	O	R

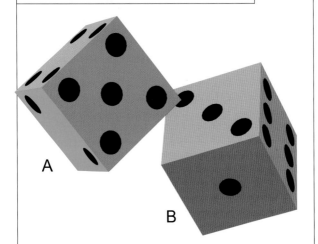

A

B

WINNING DICE

Two prisoners are spending their life sentences throwing dice. Each of them has just one old die so worn out that only three sides are legible. The three legible sides for each are shown above.

If their game awards the player who rolls the highest number, which player will win most often over the long run? (A game is not counted if either die lands with an illegible side face up.)

353

ANAGRAM

In a different order the letters *N, A, G, R* and *E* can form a meaningful word. There are two possibilities; can you find them both?

354

BASIC SHAPES

Five overlapping compositions of a triangle, a rectangle and an oval are illustrated here. Can you find the odd one out?

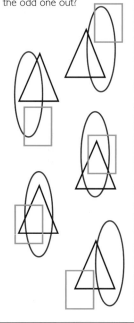

SQUARE COUNT

A teacher held up a piece of paper and asked his students to tell him how many squares they saw. They replied, "Six," which was the right answer.

The teacher held up the paper again and asked his students how many squares they saw. "Eight," they replied, again correct. So how many squares were really on the sheet? Six? Eight?

SMALL WORLD

Pick any two of the 284 million people living in the United States. If you wanted to link those two by a chain of acquaintances (a friend of a friend of a friend ...) how many people (or "links") would you need on average?

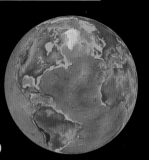

TRUE STATEMENT

Which of the three statements is true?

1) One statement here is false.

2) Two statements here are false.

3) Three statements here are false.

TUNNEL PASSAGE

Three men sat by open windows on a steam train that passed through a tunnel. All three of their faces became covered with soot. When the three passengers saw this, they started laughing at one another. Then one of them suddenly stopped because he realized that his face was also soiled.

What was his reasoning?

DRAWING BALLS

A cloth bag contains either a red ball or a blue ball. A red ball is then dropped in the bag, so now the bag has two balls.

A drawing is held, and a red ball is drawn out of the bag. Can you work out the probability of the remaining ball also being red?

LOGIC PATTERN

Each of the symbols in this matrix represents a number. The sum for each row and for three of the four columns is given. From that information, can you find the value of each symbol?

FOUR-CARD SHUFFLE

You begin a game with four cards. Two have a red pattern and two have a blue pattern, and all are blank on one side.

You shuffle the four cards and place them face down. If you pick two cards at random, what is the probability that the two cards will be the same color?

Your friend tries to convince you that the chances are ⅔ with this reasoning: there are three possibilities—two red, two blue or one of each—and since two of those are of the same color, the chances are two out of three.

Are you convinced?

ONE WORD

Can you rearrange the letters to form one word in the space provided?

REARRANGE THE TWO WORDS

| N | E | W | | D | O | O | R |

TO MAKE ONE WORD

| | | | | | | |

363

BIRTHDAY PARADOX

You want to have a party at which at least two people share the same birthday—same month and day but not necessarily the same year. If you don't know the birthdays of any of your guests, how many people do you have to invite so that the probability of two people sharing a birthday is more than 0.5? How many people do you need to invite for birthday sharing to be a practical certainty?

364

TRIPLE DUEL

Amos, Butch and Cody decide to settle their differences with a gunfight. The three cowboys draw lots for the shooting order and then take one shot each until only one is left standing.

Amos and Butch are sure shots and never miss, but Cody can hit the mark only 50 percent of the time. From that information, can you work out who has the best chance of survival?

365

COIN TOSSING

How many different outcomes are possible in one toss of two coins?

366

FLIP FRAUD

You ask a friend to flip a coin 200 times and record the outcome. When you are given the results, you want to know whether your friend really flipped the coin all those times or just faked it.

How can you check the results to see whether they are genuine?

367

LAST ALIVE

Imagine you have just become the emperor of Rome. One of your first duties is to condemn thirty-six prisoners to be eaten by lions in the arena. The lions can eat only six victims a day, and there are six hated enemies you would like to dispatch right away, but you also want to appear impartial.

The traditional Roman way to select prisoners for execution is decimation—picking every tenth person. If you have the prisoners stand in a circle, is there a way to plant your enemies at specific positions so they will be the first six selected to die?

368

DICE—EVEN-ODD

Louis Pasteur once said, "Chance favors only the prepared mind." Let's see if you have been prepared for this puzzle.

When you throw a pair of dice, what are the chances that the number that comes up will be even?

369

DIFFICULTY: ●●●●●●●●○○○

COMPLETION: ☐ TIME: _____

DICING FOR SIX

In many games you need a roll of 6 to start. One roll is generally not sufficient to get the 6. In fact, in some new games you are given a number of consecutive rolls to try to get at least one 6.

If the design of the game is to make the odds favor starting in the first round, what is the least number of rolls that players should be given?

370

DIFFICULTY: ●●●●●●●●○○○

COMPLETION: ☐ TIME: _____

DICING FOR DOUBLE SIX

You need to roll a double 6 in at least one of twenty-four throws. Are the odds in your favor?

Topology

Topology is the study of surfaces and of the continuity of one surface to another. Two figures are topologically equivalent if one can be continuously deformed (which means bending, twisting, stretching, or compressing) into another. A fundamental problem in topology is to group objects into classes of things that are topologically equivalent. You'll face that and other mind-bending topological challenges in this chapter.

371

DOT WIGGLING I

Anyone can connect all nineteen points in a closed, continuous path. But can you find the path that possesses the most wiggles? The path shown in the diagram on top has seventeen angles. Can you find another path that has seventeen angles?

TOPOLOGICAL EQUIVALENCE I

Two figures are topologically equivalent if one can be continuously deformed into another. (Continuous deformation means a shape is bent, twisted, stretched or compressed.) The figures marked a, b and c were each deformed into one of nine numbered configurations. Can you find their topological equivalents?

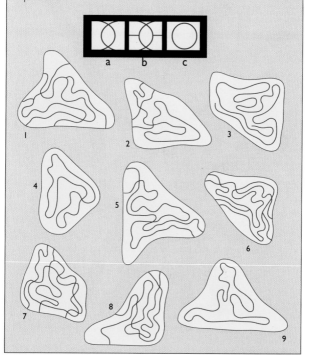

TOPOLOGY 263

DIFFICULTY: ●●●●●●●●●●

COMPLETION: □ TIME: _____

PICK-UP STICKS 2

In this puzzle each stick can be picked up only when no other stick lies on top of it. Can you work out the sequence in which to pick up all twenty sticks? Also, how many different lengths are represented?

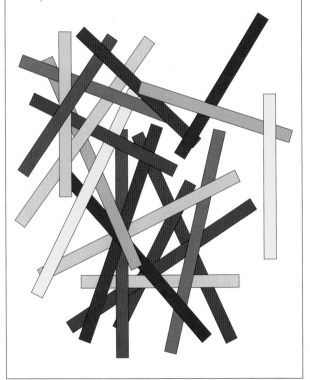

374

TOPOLOGICAL EQUIVALENCE 2

Consider that these structures are made from rubber bands and beads. Can you work out which are topologically equivalent?

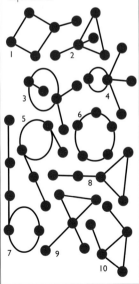

375

MAP COLORING

Can you fill in the regions on these maps using the least number of colors? Regions of the same color can meet at a point, but they cannot share a border.

376

DIFFICULTY: ●●●●●●●●●●●●
COMPLETION: ☐ TIME: _____

POLYGONAL NECKLACE

This necklace is made up of eight links, each in the form of a regular polygon, from a triangle to a decagon. Can you tell in what order the polygons are linked?

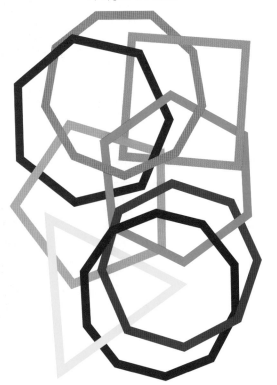

COLORING PATTERN

Say you wanted to fill in this outlined pattern without using the same color in two adjacent areas. What is the minimum number of colors you would need?

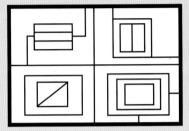

OVERLAPPING CARDS

Eight playing cards of different colors are stacked in two overlapping patterns, shown here. Can you work out the order the cards were laid down—from 8 for the bottom card to 1 for the top—for each pile?

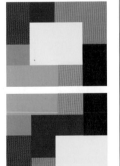

MARS COLONY

German mathematician Gerhard Ringel proposed this map problem in 1950.

Imagine that the eleven major nations on Earth have staked out territory on Mars for colonization. There is one region for each nation. To help keep the political distinctions clear, the nations insist that maps of Mars depict colonies in the same color used for mother countries on Earth maps.

Using the same color for regions that have the same number, can you fill in both maps so that no neighboring regions share a color? How many colors will you need?

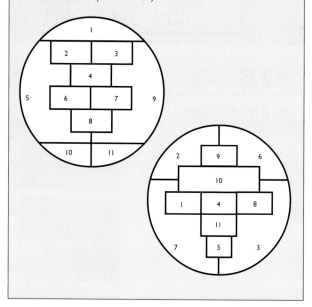

OVERLAP

Three identical rectangular frames are placed one on top of the other, as shown. The result of their intersections is seven regions. Can you work out a way to obtain twenty-five regions from the intersection of the same overlapping rectangles?

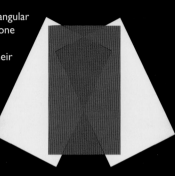

TOPOLOGY OF THE ALPHABET

Two figures are topologically equivalent if one can be continuously deformed into the other. A triangle, to the topologist's eye, is no different than a square or even a circle.

The letter E, in the font shown at right, is topologically equivalent to five other letters. Can you work out which ones?

ABCDE
FGHIJ
KLMNO
PQRST
UVWXYZ

DIFFICULTY: ●●●●●●○○○○
COMPLETION: □ TIME: _____

TOPOLOGICAL EQUIVALENCE 3

These fourteen drawings include three quartets and one pair of topologically equivalent figures.
Can you identify the solitary pair amid the quartets?

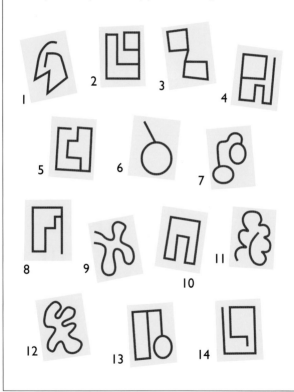

1

2

3

4

5

6

7

8

9

10

11

12

13

14

QUEENS' STANDOFF

1. Can you place ten queens on a standard chessboard so that each queen can attack only one other queen?
2. Can you place fourteen queens so that each can attack exactly two other queens?
3. Can you place sixteen queens on a standard chessboard so that each can attack only three other queens?

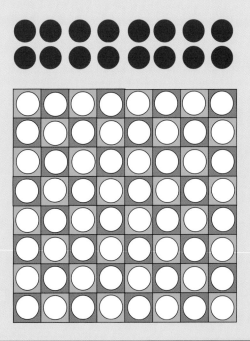

384

NO-TWO-IN-A-LINE I

Can you place the six red counters below on this six-by-six board so that no two lie on the same vertical, horizontal or diagonal line?

385

NO-TWO-IN-A-LINE 2

Can you place seven counters on the seven-by-seven board so that no two lie on the same vertical, horizontal or diagonal line?

386

NO-TWO-IN-A-LINE 3

Can you place eight counters on the eight-by-eight board so that no two are on the same vertical, horizontal or diagonal line?

This is essentially the same as asking how to place eight queens on a chessboard so that none can attack another. Can you find the twelve different solutions?

387

NO-TWO-IN-A-LINE 4

Can you place seven counters on the circles so that no two will be on the same grid line in any direction?

DIFFICULTY: ●●●●●●●○○○
COMPLETION: ☐   TIME: _____

CUTTING A CUBE

How many of the shapes shown below can be made with a single stroke of a sharp knife through a cube?

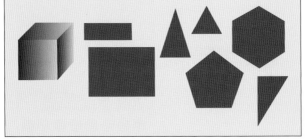

DIFFICULTY: ●●●●●○○○○○
COMPLETION: ☐   TIME: _____

MINIMAL NECKLACE

A twenty-three-bead necklace is shown here. You want to disconnect individual beads to break the necklace into smaller lengths that can then be rejoined to form every possible length from one to twenty-three beads.

Can you work out how many beads must be disconnected to accomplish this?

WATER HOSE

This garden hose is a mess. If you pull it tight at both ends, how many knots will be formed?

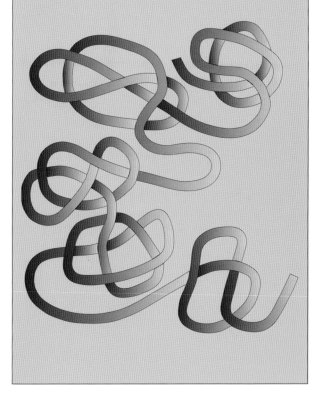

391

SHADOW KNOT

You see a length of rope on the floor before you. It is too dark to tell whether the strands pass over or under the loop at the three points of intersection. Depending on how the rope lies, pulling on the ends could tighten a knot in the rope.

Is that likely? Given that the way the rope lies is purely random, can you work out the probability that the rope is knotted rather than simply looped loosely?

392

3-D KNOT

This figure shows a three-dimensional knot composed of the least possible number of unit cubes. Each cube is the same size, there are no loose ends, and the cubes are connected across their full faces.

Can you work out the number of cubes needed to make this figure?

BEE ROOKS

Bees will attack one another if they share the same triangular row or column in the hexagonal grid. With that in mind, can you work out the greatest number of bees that can be placed on each of the four grids shown here without triggering an attack?

Can you work out the minimum number of bees needed to guard the four grids, placed so that the addition of one more bee would trigger an attack?

LOOP RELEASE

The man shown would like to release the loop, but he is unwilling to take his hand out of his pocket, take off his vest or stuff the rope into his pocket. Can you work out how he can do it?

FOLDING A NEWSPAPER

Take a sheet of ordinary newspaper and fold it in half. Easy, right?
Do you think you can fold the newspaper on itself ten more times?

SLIDING LOCK

The disk and colored blocks are embedded in a grooved plate. The blocks can slide in the grooves whenever another block isn't in the way. The disk can rotate freely and carries a square red block in its notch.

Given that information, can you find a way to slide the yellow piston from the bottom of the groove to the top of the groove? How many moves will be needed, and in what sequence?

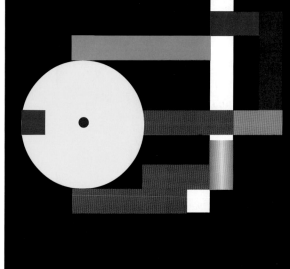

NO-THREE-IN-A-LINE I

Minimal Problem

Can you place six counters on the five-by-five board so that placing a seventh counter on any vacant circle will make a vertical, horizontal or diagonal line contain three counters?

Maximal Problem

Can you place ten counters on the five-by-five board so that placing an eleventh counter on any vacant circle will make a vertical, horizontal *and* diagonal line contain three counters?

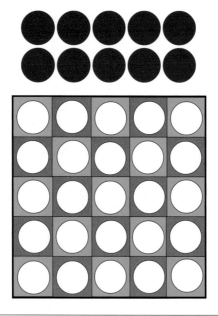

DIFFICULTY: ●●●●●●●◌◌◌
COMPLETION: ☐ TIME: _____

NO-THREE-IN-A-LINE 2

Minimal Problem

Can you place six counters on the six-by-six board so that placing a seventh counter on any vacant circle will make a vertical, horizontal or diagonal line contain three counters?

Maximal Problem

Can you place twelve counters on the six-by-six board so that placing a thirteenth counter on any open circle will make a vertical, horizontal *and* diagonal line contain three counters?

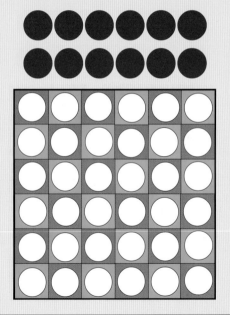

399

DIFFICULTY: ●●●●●●●○○○
COMPLETION: ☐ TIME: _____

NO-THREE-IN-A-LINE 3

Minimal Problem

Can you place eight counters on the seven-by-seven board so that placing a ninth counter on any open circle will make a vertical, horizontal or diagonal line contain three counters?

Maximal Problem

Can you place fourteen counters on the seven-by-seven board so that placing a fifteenth counter on any open circle will make a vertical, horizontal *and* diagonal line contain three counters?

400 | DIFFICULTY: ●●●●●●●●●○○
COMPLETION: ☐ TIME: _____

NO-THREE-IN-A-LINE 4

Can you place sixteen counters on the eight-by-eight board so that placing a seventeenth counter on any open circle will make a vertical, horizontal or diagonal line contain three counters?

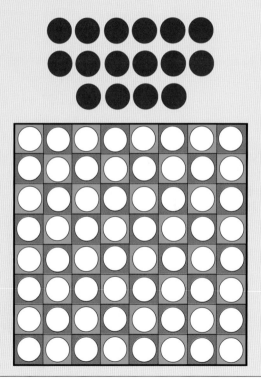

TWO-COLOR CUBES

Can you work out all the distinct ways the faces of a cube may be filled in using just two colors?

SHORTEST CATCH

The ladybug wants to reach the aphid as quickly as possible. Is the path marked the shortest route possible?

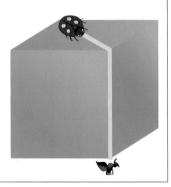

CROSSROADS

The object of this puzzle is to place seven coins or counters on the eight points of the octagonal star. Coins are placed one at a time on any unoccupied circle. But every coin that is placed must be immediately transferred to one of two other points that are connected by a straight line to the initial circle. Once moved, a coin cannot be moved again.

Although the puzzle is complicated, a simple strategy will enable you to solve it every time. Can you work it out?

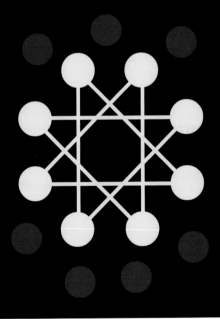

CUBE FOLD

This pattern can be folded along the creases between the squares to form a cube box. Can you work out which colors will be on opposite faces when the cube is folded?

LINK RINGS

A blacksmith has been asked to make one long chain from five three-link bits of chain. Can you find a way to do it so that he has to make just three welds?

DIFFICULTY: ●●●●●●●●○○○
COMPLETION: ☐ TIME: _____

ONE IN SEVEN

Which of the cubes cannot be made from the partially filled-in pattern?

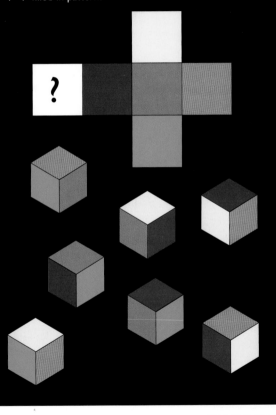

407

DIFFICULTY: ●●●●○○○○○○○○
COMPLETION: ☐ TIME: _____

TETRA-OCTA PYRAMID

The pyramid shown below is made up of regular tetrahedrons and octahedrons packed together to fill the entire volume.

If the pyramid itself is a regular tetrahedron with edges three times that of a single tetrahedral building block, how many tetrahedrons and octahedrons are needed to form the pyramid?

CUBE RINGS

This cube ring is made up of twenty-two individual cube blocks. Amazingly, it has one face and one edge, like a Möbius strip.

Can you work out the structure of the one-sided block ring made of the fewest cube blocks?

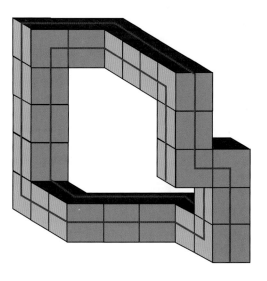

IMPOSSIBLE RECTANGLES

Of the ten figures shown here, five are identical, counting rotations but not reflections. And another set of three is identical, also counting rotations. Two of the figures are unique. Can you work out which two?

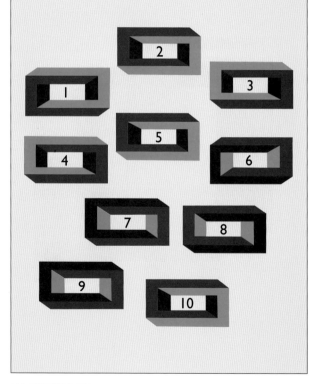

BIG CUBE THROUGH A SMALLER CUBE

Can you cut a hole through a cube that will enable a bigger cube to pass through it?

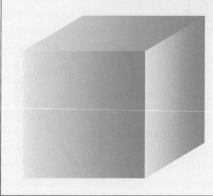

411

TWO-COLOR CORNER CUBES

In how many distinct ways can you paint the corners of a cube using only two colors? Rotations do not count as different, but reflections do.

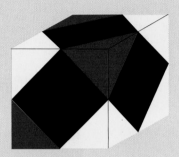

412

LINKED OR UNLINKED?

Which of the five loops must be cut so that the other loops will fall free?

413

DIFFICULTY: ●●○○○○○○○○○○
COMPLETION: ☐ TIME: _____

CUBE NETS

A cube has six faces, but does every net made up of six squares fold into a cube? Just by looking at the seven patterns here, can you tell which ones can be folded into a perfect cube box?

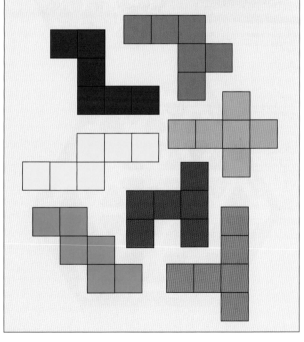

DOT WIGGLING 2

The path on top connects all twenty-seven dots with a continuous closed line that possesses twenty-six angles. Can you find another such path that possesses twenty-six angles?

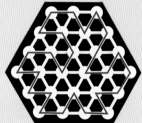

TETRA VOLUME

A tetrahedron has been sliced from a cube, as shown. Can you work out how its volume relates to that of the rest of the box?

416

HUNGRY MOUSE

Can you find a path so that the mouse eats every vegetable and exits without entering any rooms twice?

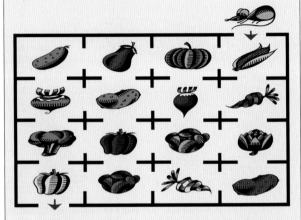

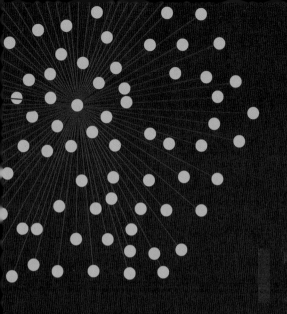

12

Science

Science is a vast and fascinating subject, but in order to solve the puzzles in this chapter, you need not be a scientific expert. Instead, you must push your brain to use its inherent understanding of scientific principles. When you think hard about how things work, you'll be surprised at how much you intuitively know—and how thrilling it is to use your mind to unlock complex scientific problems.

417

DIFFICULTY: ●●●●●●●○○○○
COMPLETION: ☐ TIME: _____

PLANETARY SCALE

Can you measure your weight anywhere in the universe using a spring scale?

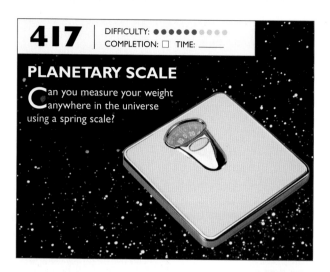

418

DIFFICULTY: ●●○○○○○○○○○
COMPLETION: ☐ TIME: _____

ASTRONAUT ON THE MOON

Do astronauts on the moon weigh the same as they do on the earth?

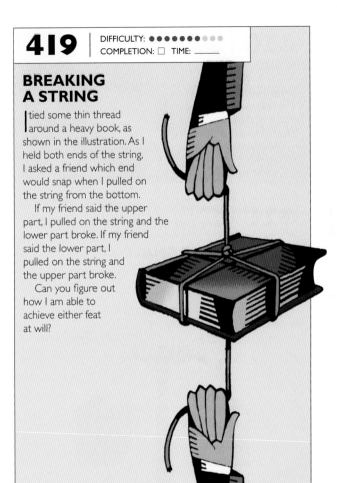

419

BREAKING A STRING

I tied some thin thread around a heavy book, as shown in the illustration. As I held both ends of the string, I asked a friend which end would snap when I pulled on the string from the bottom.

If my friend said the upper part, I pulled on the string and the lower part broke. If my friend said the lower part, I pulled on the string and the upper part broke.

Can you figure out how I am able to achieve either feat at will?

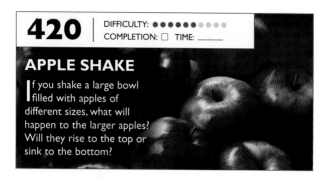

420

APPLE SHAKE

If you shake a large bowl filled with apples of different sizes, what will happen to the larger apples? Will they rise to the top or sink to the bottom?

421

BALLS BIG AND SMALL

If large steel balls are packed into a one-meter cube and small steel balls are packed into an identical cube, which weighs more?

Do you think it makes a difference that more small balls can be packed into the same space?

422

DIFFICULTY: ●●●●●●●●○○
COMPLETION: ☐ TIME: _____

RELATIVITY OF GRAVITY

Imagine you are standing in a small, sealed, windowless room. You drop two objects of different mass, and they fall with the same acceleration and hit the floor at the same time.

Given this information, can you tell for certain that you are in a room on Earth rather than in a room on a rocket that is undergoing a uniform acceleration equal to 32 feet per second per second ($32f/s^2$)?

423

DIFFICULTY: ●●●○○○○○○○
COMPLETION: ☐ TIME: _____

FALLING STONES

A large stone is 100 times heavier than a small rock, but when dropped at the same time, they fall with the same acceleration (ignoring air resistance). Why doesn't the large stone accelerate faster? Is it because of its weight, its energy, its surface area or its inertia?

PULLING STRINGS

In what two different ways can you pull a thread so that the spool rolls either toward you or away from you?

STICK-BALANCING PARADOX

You and a friend can balance a yardstick on your index fingers, as shown in the illustration. Can you work out what will happen when you both try to slide your fingers toward the middle of the stick?

What will happen if you start with both fingers in the middle and slide them toward the ends?

BOTTLED FLIES

A sealed bottle containing flies is placed on a scale. When does the scale register the heaviest weight: when the flies are resting on the bottom of the bottle, or when all the flies are in flight?

LOST RING

You have sealed the ninth of nine identical parcels of precisely equal weights, only to discover that your diamond ring has accidentally fallen into one of the packages.

You don't want to unwrap every parcel. Can you work out how to find the parcel containing the ring with just two weighings on a balance scale?

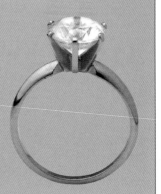

DIFFICULTY: ●●●●○○○○○○○○
COMPLETION: ☐ TIME: _____

WATERING CANS

Which watering can holds more water?

429

DIFFICULTY: ●●○○○○○○○○○○
COMPLETION: ☐ TIME: _____

BELT TRANSMISSION

If the green wheel turns clockwise, in what direction must the yellow wheel turn?

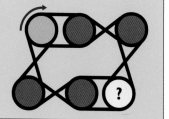

430

DIFFICULTY: ●●●●●●●○○○
COMPLETION: ☐ TIME: _____

FIVE-MINUTE EGG

You must boil an egg for exactly five minutes, but all you have is a four-minute timer and a three-minute timer. Can you work out how to use these two timers to measure five minutes?

431

DIFFICULTY: ●●○○○○○○○○
COMPLETION: ☐ TIME: _____

GEAR TRAIN I

The red cogwheel turns in a counterclockwise direction, as shown. In what direction will the blue cogwheel turn?

HOURGLASS PARADOX

A small, enclosed hourglass floats in a sealed, water-filled cylinder, as shown in the diagram. Turn the cylinder over and, surprisingly, the hourglass will not float back to the top. It will sit at the bottom until most of the sand has passed to the lower compartment. Only then will the hourglass float to the top.

Can you work out what delays the floating of the hourglass?

SATELLITE PRINCIPLE

Imagine you are standing on a 200-mile-high tower, far above the top of the atmosphere. If you throw a Frisbee hard enough, what will happen?

CLOCKWORK

Can you work out what direction the red cogwheel must turn so that the minute hand of the clock will turn clockwise?

GEAR TRAIN 2

The red cogwheel turns counterclockwise, as shown. Can you work out which way each of the two racks will move—up or down?

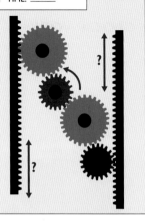

TRAPDOOR

Can you work out which way to push the rack so that the trapdoor will open?

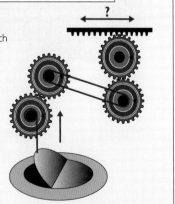

GEAR ANAGRAM

Each of the five interlocking gears possesses letters at its contact points. (The number next to the gear specifies how many teeth the gear has.) After a certain number of revolutions, the letters at the four contact points will spell out an eight-letter word, read from left to right.

Can you work out how many revolutions it will take and what the secret word is?

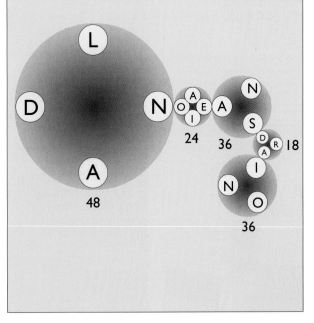

438

DIFFICULTY: ●●●●●●○○○○
COMPLETION: ☐ TIME: _____

JUGGLER

A clown who weighs 80 kilograms must carry three 10-kilogram rings across a bridge. Unfortunately, the bridge can support only 100 kilograms. The lion tamer told the clown that he could make it across if he juggled the rings—as long as at least one ring was in the air at all times, he could cross safely.

The clown followed the lion tamer's advice. Did the bridge support his weight?

439

DIFFICULTY: ●●●●○○○○○○
COMPLETION: ☐ TIME: _____

WALKING THE DOG

During his daily walk, Mr. Smith exercises his dog, Punk, by throwing a Frisbee for him to retrieve. If Mr. Smith wants Punk to run as far as possible during the walk, in what direction should he throw the Frisbee?

440

DIFFICULTY: ●●●●●●○○○○
COMPLETION: ☐ TIME: _____

JOGGING FLY

Every morning two joggers start out 10 kilometers apart, on either end of a trail. The moment the joggers start running toward the middle of the trail, a fly that sat on the head of one of the joggers flies straight toward the other; once the fly reaches the second jogger, it turns around and heads back toward the first. This back-and-forth flying continues until the two joggers meet.

If each jogger runs at a constant 5 kilometers an hour and the fly travels at 10 kilometers an hour, can you work out how many kilometers the fly covered before the joggers met?

441

DIFFICULTY: ●●●●●●○○○○
COMPLETION: ☐ TIME: _____

ROLLING THINGS

Two wooden wheels carry a 10-kilogram weight. One weight is a disk attached to the center; the other is a ring attached near the rim. If the wheels are released simultaneously on an inclined plane, which will reach the bottom first?

442

DIFFICULTY: ●●●●●●●●●○○

COMPLETION: ☐ TIME: _____

FOLDING LADDER

A folding ladder is placed on the floor with one leg supported by a stick, as shown. A bowling ball rests in the rungs near the end of the leg. A short distance away a bucket is firmly tied to the leg, and near the pivot a heavy weight rests on the leg. The idea behind the setup is a simple one: You pull the stick away, the ladder collapses, and the ball lands in the bucket.

Can such a trick work? Won't all the objects fall at the same rate?

443

DIFFICULTY: ●●●●●●●○○○
COMPLETION: ☐ TIME: _____

DROP

A woman drops a bottle from a second-story window. The bottle hits the ground at a certain speed. Can you work out from what height the bottle should be dropped to double its speed at impact?

444

DIFFICULTY: ●●●●●○○○○○
COMPLETION: ☐ TIME: _____

FROG IN THE WELL

A frog falls into the bottom of a 20-meter well. In its struggle to get out, the frog advances 3 meters up the slimy walls of the well; during the night when it rests, the frog slips back 2 meters.

Can you work out how many days it takes for the frog to escape?

445

CIRCLING WEIGHT

A ball on a string is swung in a circle at constant speed. Do the ball's velocity and acceleration stay the same? Can you work out what would happen to the ball if the string suddenly snapped?

446

GOLF BALLS

Why does a golf ball have a dimpled surface?

447 | DIFFICULTY:
COMPLETION: TIME: _____

HUMAN GYRO I

Can you work out what will happen when a boy who sits on a freely rotating stool holds a spinning bicycle tire as shown?

448 | DIFFICULTY: ●●●●●●○○○○
COMPLETION: ☐ TIME: _____

HUMAN

Can you work out what will happen when a boy who sits on a freely rotating stool holds a spinning bicycle tire as shown?

COUPLED RESONANCE PENDULUMS

Imagine connecting the bobs of two pendulums by a spring, as shown. What happens when one of the pendulums is released? Do the interconnected pendulums eventually have the same amount of energy?

MARBLE LIFTING MAGIC

Can you lift a marble off a table using only a wineglass?

451

DIFFICULTY: ●●●●●●●○○○
COMPLETION: ☐ TIME: _____

PECKING WOODPECKER

You may have seen a variation of this toy. Begin with the woodpecker at the top of the rod. If you lift back the woodpecker and release it, the woodpecker will peck the rod and slowly descend to the bottom. Can you explain this behavior?

452

DIFFICULTY: ●●●●●●●○○○
COMPLETION: ☐ TIME: _____

ROTATING BODIES

A metal disc, a solid cone and a closed chain are suspended from strings, as shown. Their strings are then rotated rapidly. Can you work out the position of the suspended bodies as they rotate?

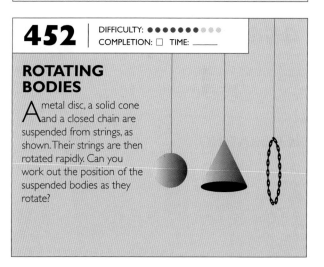

453

HUMAN GYRO 3

A boy sitting on a freely rotating stool holds a spinning bicycle tire vertically with both hands as shown. Can you work out what he should do so that his stool will begin to turn left? Will pushing the handle forward with his right hand and backward with his left accomplish this?

454

ICE SKATING

A figure skater spins on the ice with her arms held wide open. What happens when she brings her hands to her chest?

CENTRIPETAL FORCE

Rotating rides, such as the rotating vertical cylinder shown here, are popular at carnivals. Riders stand with their backs to the wall as the cylinder begins to spin. When the maximum spin rate is reached, the floor drops away. Amazingly, the riders remain stuck to the wall.

Can you work out why this occurs?

456

WHO FIRED THE FIRST SHOT?

Look at the scene as a detective would: The three men each fired a shot. The holes from their shots match the colored dots on their hats. From this information, can you work out who fired the first shot—Joe, John or Jim?

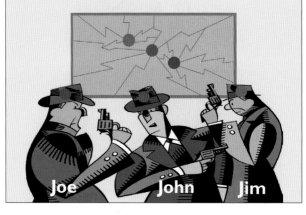

457

UP AND DOWN

A baseball is tossed in the air. Which takes longer, its flight up or its drop back down?

458

DIFFICULTY: ●●●●○○○○○○
COMPLETION: ☐ TIME: _____

EXPANDING HOLE

A steel washer with a hole in the center is heated until the metal expands by 1 percent. Will the hole get larger or smaller or remain unchanged?

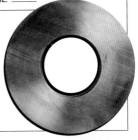

459

DIFFICULTY: ●●●●●●○○○○
COMPLETION: ☐ TIME: _____

TREES AND BRANCHES

Can you work out why a tree takes on the form of a branched structure like the one on the right rather than a radial structure such as the one on the left?

460

BERNOULLI'S SURPRISE

Two lightweight beach balls are suspended a short distance from each other, as shown. Can you guess what will happen if you blow air between the two balls?

461

BATH

Imagine you are in a bathtub checking to see how much weight your toy duck can carry before it sinks. You place a heavy metal ring on the duck, and it doesn't sink. Then the ring slips off and falls to the bottom of the tub.

When the ring falls, does the water level in the tub go up, go down or stay the same?

462

DIFFICULTY: ●●●●●●○○○○
COMPLETION: ☐ TIME: _____

AIRPLANE FLIGHT

Why is the top of an airplane wing curved?

463

DIFFICULTY: ●●●●●●○○○○
COMPLETION: ☐ TIME: _____

AIR JET

Put a Ping-Pong ball inside a small funnel. Then tip your head back and blow as hard as you can. Rather than being blown to the ceiling, the ball remains suspended in the air. The harder you blow, the higher it will float above the funnel. Can you work out what causes such strange behavior?

ASCENDING BALL

Will the time it takes for a Ping-Pong ball to rise to the top of a cylinder of water be different if the water in the cylinder is still or if it is swirling around?

BLOWING CANDLES

What happens when you blow between two burning candles?

TEA WITH MILK

You have two glasses, one exactly half full of tea, the other exactly half full of milk. Take a teaspoon of milk from the glass and stir it into the tea. Then take a teaspoon of the tea-milk mixture and stir that into the glass with the milk.

Can you tell whether there is more milk in the tea than there is tea in the milk? Or is there more tea in the milk than milk in the tea?

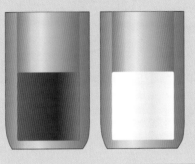

FALLING RAINDROPS

Which raindrops fall faster—the large ones on the small ones?

468

DIFFICULTY: ●●●●●●●●○○○
COMPLETION: ☐ TIME: _____

ICEBERG

A bathtub holding an iceberg is filled to the brim with water. Can you tell what will happen when the iceberg melts?

469

DIFFICULTY: ●●●●●●●○○○
COMPLETION: ☐ TIME: _____

MUSICAL TUBE

Wave a flexible corrugated tube around in a circle, and it will make a sound. Can you explain why?

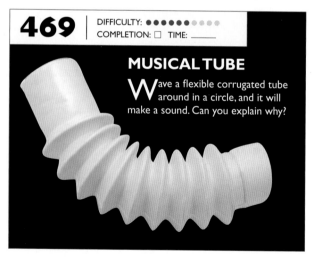

470

DIFFICULTY: ●●●●●●●○○○
COMPLETION: ☐ TIME: _____

FINGER IN THE GLASS

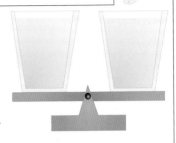

Two glasses filled with water are balanced on a scale, as shown. What happens to the scale when you stick your finger in one of the glasses? Will that side of the balance tip, as if it were heavier?

How would the result change if your finger were made of heavy metal?

471

DIFFICULTY: ●●●●●○○○○○
COMPLETION: ☐ TIME: _____

CORK IN A GLASS

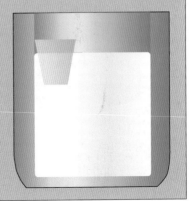

You have no doubt observed that a cork will always drift over to the side of a water glass and stay there. Can you think of a way to make the cork float in the middle of the glass without touching either the cork or the glass?

472

DIFFICULTY: ●●●●●●●●○○○

COMPLETION: ☐ TIME: _____

MAGNIFIER IN WATER

Will a magnifying glass enlarge the image of the knife more if the lens is placed underwater?

473

DIFFICULTY: ●●●●○○○○○○
COMPLETION: ☐ TIME: _____

PENNIES IN A GLASS

Fill a glass with water completely up to the rim. Then slip a penny into the glass—the water will not overflow. Can you guess how many pennies you can slip into the glass before the water spills over the edge?

474

DIFFICULTY: ●●●●●○○○○○
COMPLETION: ☐ TIME: _____

MARIONETTE'S CONTAINER

A cylinder of water has three holes, spaced as shown in the diagram. A faucet runs into the cylinder to supply enough water to keep the water level constant.

When the holes are unplugged, water will stream continuously from the three holes. Can you work out which stream will shoot out the farthest?

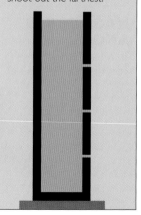

475

DIFFICULTY: ●●●●●●●○○○
COMPLETION: ☐ TIME: _____

AIRPLANE SHADOW

An airplane flying at several thousand feet casts a shadow on the ground. Will it be larger, smaller or the same size as the airplane?

476

DIFFICULTY: ●●●●○○○○○○
COMPLETION: ☐ TIME: _____

MAGNIFYING ANGLE

If you view an angle of 15 degrees through a lens that magnifies every dimension by three, can you work out how large the angle will appear?

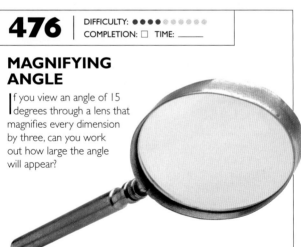

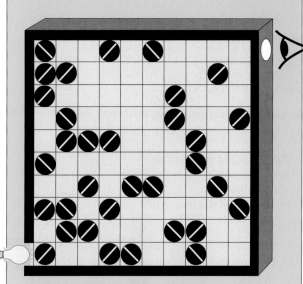

SUPER PERISCOPE

If you rotate ten of the double-sided mirrors by 90 degrees each, you will be able to see the reflection of the lightbulb from the porthole in the top right-hand corner. Can you work out which ten mirrors must be moved?

FULL-LENGTH MIRROR

Can you work out the minimum height of a mirror that lets you see a full head-to-toe view of yourself?

FASHION MIRROR

The model stands 2 meters from the dresser mirror and holds a hand mirror half a meter behind her head. How far behind the dresser mirror is the image of the red flower in her hair?

13

Bonus Round

This finale of neuron-strengthening fun brings together all of the elements you've explored in the preceding chapters. To master these puzzles, you'll rely on the creativity, logic, and insight you've worked to develop. When you've solved them all, you'll experience the thrill that comes from having stretched your brain in so many new and different directions.

480

DIFFICULTY: ●●●●●●●●●○○○
COMPLETION: □ TIME: _____

EXHIBITION WIRING

An architect is examining his design for the placement of the electrical outlets in an exhibition hall. The hall is divided into identical unit blocks, and the client needs each intersection to be no more than three blocks from an electrical outlet.

His initial design, shown here, used twenty-five electrical outlets, but the architect is certain that there is a more economical solution. Is he right? Can you find the design that provides the fewest number of outlets yet puts no intersection more than three blocks from an outlet?

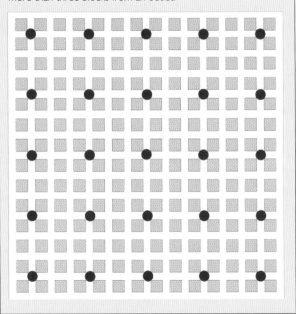

DIFFICULTY: ●●●●●●●○○○

COMPLETION: ☐ TIME: _____

CRAWLING CENTIPEDE

A centipede sits at the top corner of a three-dimensional solid structure, as shown. Can you find a route along the edges for the bug so that it visits each corner once and only once while not traveling along any edge more than once? (Note that its path will not include every edge.)

DIFFICULTY: ●●●●○○○○○○

COMPLETION: ☐ TIME: _____

WINNING HORSES

If seven horses have entered a race, how many different ways can the first three places be filled?

483

DIFFICULTY: ●●●●●●●●●○○
COMPLETION: ☐ TIME: _____

CIRCLE DIVISIONS

Using just a compass and a ruler, can you divide this circle into eight regions of equal area?

484

DIFFICULTY: ●●●●○○○○○○○○
COMPLETION: ☐ TIME: _____

CABLE CONNECTION

A telephone cable has twenty wires—five in each of four different colors. If you are working in total darkness, how many wires must you grab to ensure that you have one of each color?

485

DIFFICULTY: ●●●●●●●●●○○○

COMPLETION: ☐ TIME: _____

OVERLAPPING POLYGONS

For each of the sets of overlapping shapes, can you work out which is larger: the sum of the uncovered red areas or the uncovered blue area in the middle? Refer to the box to figure out the relative sizes of the shapes.

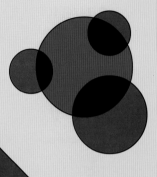

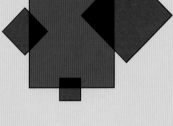

Squares	Circles	Equilateral Triangles
Sides: 2 units	Radius: 2 units	Sides: 2 units
Sides: 3 units	Radius: 2 units	Sides: 2 units
Sides: 6 units	Radius: 3.5 units	Sides: 4 units
Sides: 8 units	Radius: 4.5 units	Sides: 4 units
		Sides: 6 units

486

DIFFICULTY: ●●●●●●●●●●○○
COMPLETION: ☐ TIME: _____

COMBINATION LOCK

The lock shown here is opened by selecting the correct nonrepeating three-letter combination. If a bank robber has one guess at opening the lock, what are the chances that he'll guess correctly?

487

DIFFICULTY: ●●●●●●○○○○
COMPLETION: ☐ TIME: _____

MY CLASS

In a class of fifteen boys, fourteen have blue eyes, twelve have black hair, eleven are overweight and ten are tall. Can you work out how many tall, overweight, black-haired, blue-eyed boys there must be?

488

DIFFICULTY: ●●●●●●○○○○
COMPLETION: ☐ TIME: _____

WALKING DOGS

Beatrice has six dogs to walk. If she walks them two at a time, how many different pairs of dogs can she take out?

489

DIFFICULTY: ●●●●●●●●●○
COMPLETION: ☐ TIME: _____

MAGIC GRID MATRIX I

Can you divide this matrix along the grid lines into sixteen identical parts? No two parts may have the same numbers, and the sum of the numbers in each part must total 34.

2	3	13	16	3	2	14	15
5	8	10	11	4	9	10	11
11	10	9	4	13	16	1	2
16	13	4	1	14	7	9	6
4	5	10	13	5	8	10	11
3	6	11	16	2	14	8	10
12	10	9	3	11	5	3	15
15	13	4	2	16	12	5	1

490

DIFFICULTY: ●●●●●●●●○○
COMPLETION: ☐ TIME: _____

LICENSE PLATES

In many countries automobile license plates take the form shown here: one letter, followed by three numbers, followed by three letters.

In such a country how many different license plates are possible?

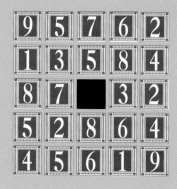

491

DIFFICULTY: ●●●●●●●●○○
COMPLETION: ☐ TIME: _____

MAGIC GRID MATRIX 2

Examine this matrix of numbers. Can you divide it into eight parts in such a way that the digits in each part will add up to the same total?

9	5	7	6	2
1	3	5	8	4
8	7	■	3	2
5	2	8	6	4
4	5	6	1	9

DODECAHEDRON EDGE COLORING

How many colors do you need to color each segment of this diagram in such a way that no two segments of the same color meet at a junction?

EDGE COLORING PATTERN

Imagine you want to color in the lines of this diagram in such a way that no two lines of the same color meet at an endpoint (shown as circles). How many different colors will you need?

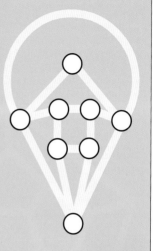

THREE-DIGIT NUMBER

A toy robot has a three-digit electronic display on its front. The only digits it can display are 1, 2 and 3. Can you work out how many different numbers the robot can display?

1 2 3

DIFFICULTY: ●●●●○○○○○○

COMPLETION: □ TIME: _____

COUNTING LETTERS

Read the following sentence:

FINISHED FILES ARE THE RESULT OF YEARS OF SCIENTIFIC STUDY COMBINED WITH THE EXPERIENCE OF YEARS.

Now read it again, this time counting every *F* you see. How many did you find?

DIFFICULTY: ●●●●○○○○○○

COMPLETION: □ TIME: _____

EQUAL AREAS

This diagram shows three pairs of quarter circles in contact with each other, as well as a number of isolated quarter circles of various sizes. It turns out that the sum of the area of each pair of quarter circles is equal to the area of one of the single quarter circles shown. Can you work out which quarter circle goes with which pair? Can you guess which geometric property ensures that the areas are exactly equal?

497

FIBONACCI RABBITS

In 1202 Leonardo Fibonacci, a twenty-seven-year-old Italian mathematician, published a book called *Liber Abaci*. In that groundbreaking work, he wrote the following puzzle:

Every month a breeding pair of rabbits (one male, one female) produces one new pair of rabbits—also one male, one female. That new pair begins breeding two months later. How many pairs of rabbits can be produced from a single pair of rabbits in one year, assuming no rabbits die and every pair has one male and one female?

498

AN ARRAY OF SOLDIERS

Each of eleven army units (represented here by the green squares) has an identical number of soldiers. If you add one general to the total number, the soldiers can be rearranged to form a single perfect array of fighting personnel.

What's the minimum number of soldiers that must be in each army unit? How many soldiers—including the general—are in the array?

499

MATHEMAGIC HONEYCOMB

Can you place the numbers 1 through 9 in this honeycomb so that, for any given hexagon, the sum of the numbers in the adjacent hexagons will be a multiple of that hexagon's number? For example, if a hexagon contains a 5, the adjacent hexes must total 5, 10, 15, 25 and so on.

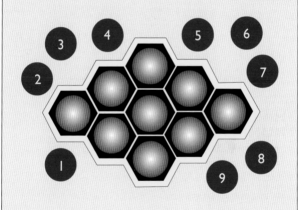

500

DIFFICULTY: ●●●●●●●●●○○
COMPLETION: ☐ TIME: _____

HAILSTONE NUMBERS

Think of a number. If it is odd, triple it and add 1; if it is even, divide it by 2. Apply this rule to each new number you obtain. Can you see what eventually happens?

Starting with 1, you get: 1, 4, 2, 1, 4, 2, 1, 4, 2 and so on.

Starting with 2 gives you: 2, 1, 4, 2, 1, 4, 2, 1, 4 and so on.

Starting with 3: 3, 10, 5, 16, 8, 4, 2, 1, 4, 2, 1 and so on.

It quickly becomes apparent that the above sequences get stuck in a loop of 1-4-2-1-4-2. But will every sequence run into that inescapable routine? Test your idea by starting with 7.

TRUTH AND MARRIAGE

The king has two daughters—the virtuous Amelia, who always tells the truth, and the wicked Leila, who always lies. One of them is married, and one of them is not—but the king has kept the details of the marriage a secret, even down to which of the daughters is wedded.

To find a suitable mate for the other daughter, the king has organized a joust. The winner gets to name which of the daughters he wants to marry; if she is available, they will wed the next day. The man who wins asks the king if he may talk to the daughters. The king says he may ask one of the daughters one question, but it can be no more than three words long.

What question should he ask?

HOTEL INFINITY

This problem is a favorite introduction to the weirdness of infinite numbers:

You are the manager of the Hotel Infinity, an inn that has an infinite number of rooms. No matter how crowded the hotel is, you know that you can always make room for one more guest: you simply move the person in room 1 to room 2, the person in room 2 to room 3, the person in room 3 to room 4 and so on. After all the guests have been moved, you check the new guest into room 1.

Unfortunately, just as you are about to go off-duty, a group of people arrive for a convention. The topic must be very popular, because there are an infinite number of new guests. If you already *have* an infinite number of guests, how can you accommodate the newcomers?

503

TRUTH CITY

You are on your way to Truth City, where the inhabitants always tell the truth. At one point you reach a fork in the road, with one branch leading to Truth City and the other leading to Lies City, where the citizens are all liars. The road signs at the junction are, as you can imagine, confusing, but there is a man standing there from whom you can ask directions. The only problem is, you don't know where he is from—the city where everyone always gives the right answer or the city where everyone lies.

If you have time to ask him only one question, what question will ensure that you will be headed in the right direction?

504

THREE DICE

You see three faces on each of three dice, for a total of nine faces. If the sum of the dots on each die is different, and you see a total of forty dots altogether, then can you work out which faces must be visible on each die?

NONTRANSITIVE DICE

The mathematical property of transitivity states that if A is greater than B, and B is greater than C, then A is greater than C. But certain games appear to flout this logic. One common nontransitive game is "Rock, Paper, Scissors," the children's game that displays circular logic: Scissors cut paper, paper wraps rock, rock breaks scissors.

A special set of dice, shown here, also displays this nontransitive logic. If you play a two-person betting game with these dice, always allow your opponent to select his or her die first. No matter which die your opponent chooses, you can select a die that will give you an advantage. Can you work out how?

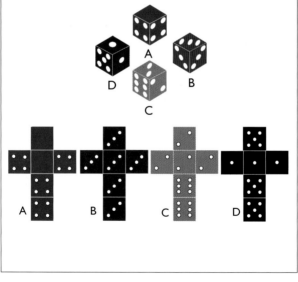

506

TRUTH, LIES AND IN BETWEEN

There are three types of people in the city of Las Wages: those who always tell the truth, those who always lie and those who alternate between lying and truth telling. If you meet an inhabitant on the streets of Las Wages and can ask only two questions, what two questions will enable you to determine what sort of person he or she is?

507

LINKED OR NOT?

Could the elements of the structure below be separated without making a cut?

FLIPPING COIN GAME

Two boys play a simple game: They take turns flipping a coin, and the first to throw "heads" wins. Can you work out whether one player can gain an advantage even if the coin is fair?

TRIANGLES IN A CUBE

Choose any three corners of a cube at random. Can you work out the chances that those points will form a right triangle?

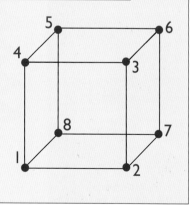

510

PYTHAGOREAN HEXAGONS

A set of regular hexagons with sides 3, 4 and 5 is extended on the sides of a right triangle. This seems to suggest that the Pythagorean theorem can be extended beyond squares and is valid for hexagons as well. Is that really the case?

A related problem was posed by American mathematician James Schmerl. He noted that a hexagon of side 5 can be dissected so that the pieces can form two smaller hexagons, one of side 3 and one of side 4. What is the smallest number of pieces that will accomplish this?

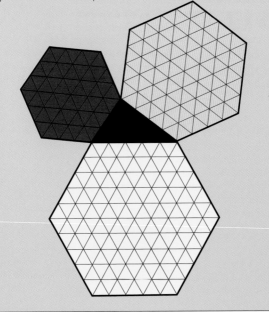

BIRD NEST

Seven birds live in a nest. They are very organized and send three birds out each day in search of food. After seven days every pair of birds will have been in exactly one of the daily foraging missions. For example, on the first day birds 1, 2 and 3 go out; that means the pairs 1-2, 1-3 and 2-3.

Can you work out how every pair can be so matched over the course of a week?

MINIMAL ROUTES

Three, four and five towns are represented by red points on the three maps shown here. For each map, can you draw the shortest possible road system that links all the towns?

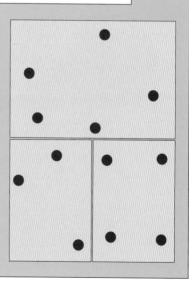

SEPARATING GHOSTS

Can you separate the fifteen ghosts into fifteen private compartments just by moving the five straight lines?

THE TOSS OF THE DIE

If you toss a die six times, what are the chances that all six faces will turn up?

DIFFICULTY: ●●●●●●●●●○○○
COMPLETION: ☐ TIME: _____

LINKED TUBES

Several tubes of various shapes are linked in such a way that liquid can pass from one to another. The network of tubes is connected to a reservoir of water, at left. If the reservoir is opened and the water flows into the tubes, can you work out what the water level will be in each tube?

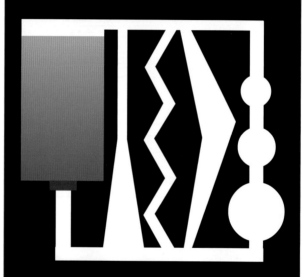

516

PROGRESSING SQUARES

Start with a small square of side 1. Employ the diagonal of that square as the side of a second square. Employ the diagonal of the second square as the side of a third square. Continue in this manner to create an infinite progression of squares.

Without measuring, can you work out what the length of the sides of the eleventh square in the series will be?

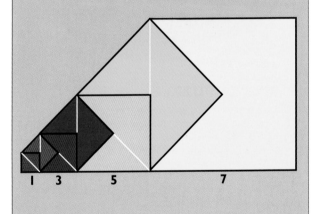

1   3   5   7

THE LAST PUZZLE

This last challenge was very carefully selected. The solution requires thinking, concentration, creativity, logic, insight and attention to the smallest detail. Enjoy!

Two Russian mathematicians meet on a plane.

"If I remember correctly, you have three sons," says Ivan. "What are their ages today?"

"The product of their ages is thirty-six," says Igor, "and the sum of their ages is exactly today's date."

"I'm sorry, Igor," Ivan says after a minute, "but that doesn't tell me the ages of your boys."

"Oh, I forgot to tell you, my youngest son has red hair."

"Ah, now it's clear," Ivan says. "I now know exactly how old your three sons are."

How did Ivan figure out the ages?

SOLUTIONS

CHAPTER I SOLUTIONS

1 The Roman numeral for seven (VII) can be made by cutting the Roman numeral for twelve (XII) in half horizontally.

2 16,807 measures of flour. That's 7 × 7 × 7 × 7 × 7. This puzzle, which comes from the ancient Egyptian "Rhind Papyrus," was written by the scribe Ahmes in 1850 B.C. Perhaps the world's oldest puzzle, it has inspired a great many variations over the thousands of years since its creation.

3 The frames are exactly identical. Because the frames are three-dimensional, they can be arranged in a nontransitive way so that A is inside B, B is inside C, and C is inside A.

4 Door number 5 is the right answer. In many instances people choose a door that is more square than the original. That is because the background figure often influences one's perception of the door's shape.

5 The egg. The riddle does not specify that the eggs in question are chicken eggs and, according to paleontologists, reptiles and dinosaurs existed long before birds and chickens. Fossilized eggs dating back one hundred million years have been uncovered. Thus it can be said that eggs came before chickens.

6

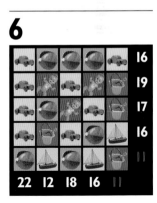

7 The winning sequence is yellow, orange, red, pink, violet, green, sage, blue, and lavender.

8

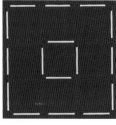

9 The choices offer identical odds. But in a psychological experiment, about four in ten people preferred the single draw and held to this view even when the other choice was altered to provide fifty draws from the box of 100.

10

$$1 + 2 + 3 + 4 + 5 = 15$$
$$1 \times 2 \times 3 \times 4 \times 5 = 120$$

11 The number 2,520 is obviously divisible by 5 and 10. But since all five of the numbers are single-digit, 10 is excluded. So the third number must be 5.

Adding the known numbers $(8 + 1 + 5)$ gives us 14. Since $30 - 14 = 16$, the total of the remaining two numbers must be 16.

Multiplying the known numbers $(8 \times 1 \times 5)$ gives us 40. Since $2,520 / 40 = 63$, the product of the two remaining numbers must be 63.

Only 9 and 7 can be added to make 16 and multiplied together to make 63.

So the answer is 5, 7 and 9.

12

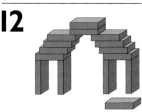

The key to constructing the bridge is to set up two dominoes as temporary supports, as shown in the illustration above. When enough dominoes have been placed to give the structure its overall stability, the supports can be removed and placed on top.

13 If the drawer contained socks, then you would need to select only four to get a matching pair. But gloves have an attribute that socks don't: handedness. It is not enough to have two gloves that are the same color—they must be of complementary handedness. So to ensure that you have one pair of gloves, you must select one more than the number of gloves of one-handedness, or twelve. Assuming that you can distinguish in the dark between right- and left-handed gloves, you may need to select only eleven.

14 The outlines of the six overlapping squares for one six-by-six square, six three-by-three squares, three two-by-two squares and eight one-by-one squares—eighteen squares altogether.

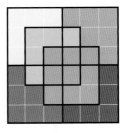

15 There are sixteen possible combinations of choices for the firing of the four lasers. Four combinations will form a closed energy field around the man:

left, left, left and left
left, right, left and right
right, left, right and left
right, right, right and right

The probability of success, then, is one in four.

16 The trick here is looking at the way the books are lined up. The bookworm eats through only the front cover of volume 1, all of volumes 2, 3 and 4, and only the back cover of volume 5. The total distance is 19 centimeters.

17 The first step you must take to solve the problem is to find the number of combinations of three colors you can make from five colors. Plugging the values into a general formula for the number of combinations gives you:

$$5!/(3! \times (5 - 3)!) =$$
$$(5 \times 4 \times 3 \times 2 \times 1) /$$
$$(3 \times 2 \times 1 \times (2 \times 1)) =$$
$$120/12 = 10$$

That result tells us there are ten possible combinations of three colors out of five. But the number of combinations tells us nothing about the order in which the colors are placed on the mask. The different orders in which the three colors can be painted on the mask is 3! ($3 \times 2 \times 1$), or six for each color combination. That means there is a total of sixty possible ways the mask could be painted using three colors out of five.

---

18 If the treasure were buried on the orange island, then all the statements would be false. And if the treasure were buried on the purple island, then all the statements would be true. But if the treasure were buried on

the yellow island, then only the statement for the purple island would be false. Therefore, the treasure is on the yellow island.

---

19 Your friend is wrong. Because the odds for each coin is independent of the others, there are in fact two possible outcomes for a single coin, four possible outcomes for two coins and eight possible outcomes for three coins:

1	2	3
H	H	H
H	H	T
H	T	H
H	T	T
T	H	H
T	H	T
T	T	H
T	T	T

In only two tosses out of eight will the coins land all heads or all tails.

20

---

21 The hostages can easily separate themselves. One of the hostages grabs his rope with both hands so that a loose, untwisted loop is made in his rope on the other side of his partner's rope. Then he tucks the loop through the circle of rope around his partner's wrist; as you'll soon discover, it's only possible to keep the rope untwisted by moving toward one wrist, not the other. Next, he moves the loop up toward his partner's fingers. When the first hostage then passes the loop over his partner's hand and tucks the loop back through the rope, they are free.

22 $6 + \frac{6}{6} = 7$

23   The answer is a man. A man crawls on all fours in the morning of his life (when he is a baby), walks upright in middle age, and uses a cane in old age.

24   The solution uses the Pythagorean theorem (the square of the length of the hypotenuse of a right triangle equals the sum of the squares of the lengths of the other two sides) to calculate the length from the lower front left-hand corner of the chest to the upper back right-hand corner. First the diagonal of the base is determined to be 50 centimeters; then that length and the height of the chest can be used to calculate the maximum length through the box. That turns out to be 70.7 centimeters—just long enough for the sword to fit!

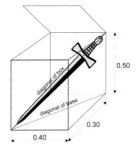

25   It can't be done. If you start drawing a line outside the black closed line and cross it an odd number of times, you will end up inside the black line. To close the new line, you must intersect the black line, making an even number of intersections. Not only are nine intersections impossible, all odd numbers of intersections are impossible.

26 With two statements there are four possible combinations of truth or falsehood:

> true/true
> true/false
> false/true
> false/false

The first combination can't be right because at least one of the statements is false. The second and third can't be right either because if one of the statements is false, it's impossible for the other to be true. The only logically consistent possibility is that they both lied. That means Mister Ladybug has the yellow dots and Miss Ladybug has the red dots.

27 The larger rug covers exactly 25 percent of the smaller one. The proof of this is shown in the diagram below.

28 There were six people at the meeting. Each person shook hands five times, but that makes for fifteen handshakes, not thirty, since each shake was shared by two people.

29 Five, as illustrated below.

30 The total number of possible permutations in a seven-digit phone number is seven factorial (7!, or 7 × 6 × 5 × 4 × 3 × 2 × 1), which equals 5,040. So the probability of any given combination being the right phone number is 1 in 5,040, or about .02 percent.

31 In each row the yellow wedges add up to make a complete square.

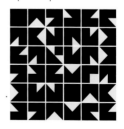

32 Change the word *man* to *person*. Otherwise, it is possible that the man has a wife and many daughters and that one of them knocked on the door.

33 Since the nine bananas, nine oranges and nine apples in the three fruit baskets together cost $4.05, the cost of one of each fruit should cost just one-ninth of that, or $0.45. (There's no need to know that apples are 10 cents each, bananas are 20 cents each and oranges are 15 cents each.)

34

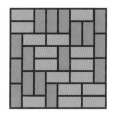

35 The maximum number of attempts can be found by adding:

$$8 + 7 + 6 + 5 + 4 + 3 + 2 + 1$$
$$= 36 \text{ attempts}$$

36 You can write four numbers:

a. $2^{2^2} = 2^4 = 16$, the smallest number

b. 222

c. $22^2 = 484$

d. $2^{22} = 4,194,304$, the largest number

Using powers is an efficient way to write very large or very small numbers. Raising a number to a power simply means multiplying it by itself as many times as is indicated by the power. So:

$$2^{22} = 2 \times 2$$
$$= 4,194,304$$

37 Based on her remark, we know that Miss Blue's dress is either pink or green. Since the woman who replied to her was wearing a green dress, that means Miss Blue must be wearing pink. That leaves the blue dress for Miss Green and the green dress for Miss Pink.

38 If you shake one of the coins out of the bank labeled "15¢," you can figure out how to correctly label all the banks. Since you know that the bank is mislabeled, it cannot hold 15 cents—instead, the bank contains either two dimes or two nickels. The coin that drops out will tell you what the other coin is. Say the answer is two dimes; that leaves you with three nickels and a dime between the two remaining banks, one labeled "20¢" and one labeled "10¢." Since the bank labeled "10¢" cannot have two nickels in it—because it is mislabeled—it must contain a nickel and a dime, and the other bank must have the two nickels.

39 Card number 3 is not found in the colored pattern.

40

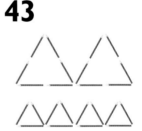

41 When overlapped, the strips can create a six-pointed star.

42 Four cuts, as shown, will be sufficient. Notice that the lengths are equal to the place numbers in the base 2, or binary, number system.

1 2 4   8   16

43

44 The answer is yes. As pictured, it is possible to place a maximum of thirty-two knights on the board so that each piece can attack one and only one other piece.

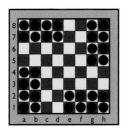

47

48

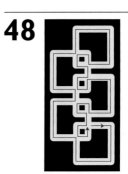

45 One in six. Three hats can be distributed among three people in six different ways: ABC, ACB, BAC, BCA, CAB, CBA.

46 The five numbers between 1 and 100 that have twelve factors:

60: 1, 2, 3, 4, 5, 6, 10, 12, 15, 20, 30, 60

72: 1, 2, 3, 4, 6, 8, 9, 12, 18, 24, 36, 72

84: 1, 2, 3, 4, 6, 7, 12, 14, 21, 28, 42, 84

90: 1, 2, 3, 5, 6, 9, 10, 15, 18, 30, 45, 90

96: 1, 2, 3, 4, 6, 8, 12, 16, 24, 32, 48, 96

CHAPTER 2 SOLUTIONS

49

50 In the geometry of Gridlock City, the shortest route that links all four points is twenty blocks long. And there are 10,000 different routes that you could take that are that short.

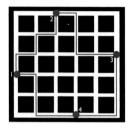

51 In Flatland a law was passed requiring women to constantly twist and turn. In that way they would always be visible.

52

53 The sixteen views are combined correctly in the table:

A/15	E/10	I/14	M/13
B/11	F/12	J/7	N/1
C/8	G/16	K/9	O/4
D/6	H/3	L/2	P/5

The multiview problems combine spatial awareness with logic—the ability to visualize in three-dimensional views.

In fact, the overhead views and front views given correspond fairly well to what architects call a plan and front elevation. The plan represents the shape as laid out horizontally on the ground; the elevation is a front view that is derived exactly and immediately from the dimensions of the plan.

Other elevations derived by architects in the same way are those of the remaining sides of the building, each seen as a direct face-on-view, with no perspective.

54

55 The last two tiles don't follow the rule.

56 The red letters are the capital letters in the alphabet that have only vertical symmetry. The blue letters are the capitals that have only horizontal symmetry.

57 The blue letters are the capital letters that have both horizontal and vertical symmetry. The red letters are asymmetrical.

58

59 The parallelogram has no symmetry axes. The circle has an infinite number of symmetry axes.

60 The symmetries of the capital letters can be categorized as follows:

1. Letters that are symmetrical only in the vertical plane: A, M, T, U, V, W, Y

2. Letters that are symmetrical only in the horizontal plane: B, C, D, E, K

3. Letters symmetrical in both the vertical and horizontal planes: H, I, O, X

4. Letters that possess only rotational symmetry: N, S, Z

5. Asymmetric letters: F, G, J, L, P, Q, R

61 The red letters are asymmetrical. The blue letters have a twofold rotational symmetry. Although some shapes—and letters—have no bilateral symmetry, they still possess rotational symmetry.

62 The cube has three fourfold axes of rotational symmetry, four threefold axes and six twofold axes. In general, having a certain number-fold of rotational axes means that if you rotate the object through part of a full rotation equal to the inverse of that number (for example, one-third rotation for a three-fold axis), you get a figure identical to the original.

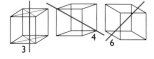

63

64

65

66

A solution with seven triangles is illustrated.

In general, what is the largest number of nonoverlapping triangles that can be enclosed by n straight line segments? Trial and error will quickly lead you to the discovery that for $n = 3, 4, 5$ and 6, the maximum number of triangles enclosed is one, two, five and seven, respectively. When the problem reaches $n = 7$, trial and error no longer provides the easy answer. And the general problem for *n* of any number has yet to be solved.

67 You can check with your own randomly drawn lines, but the intersections will always align. That surprising result is known as Pappus's theorem.

68 The sets of straight lines will blur into concentric circles of different sizes. That baffling result is due to an optical illusion. You no doubt have seen such an illusion before, but you may not know why it works. Don't feel bad: even scientists who study human perception are not sure why straight lines can be perceived as circles.

The most important element of the illusion is something you don't really see—the center point around which the rest of the disc revolves. The distance from that center point to the middle of the line will give you the approximate radius of the circle you see when the turntable begins its motion.

1   2   3   4

69

70 An eleven-triangle solution is illustrated.

71 A fifteen-triangle solution is shown.

72 There is only one convex polygon: the hexagon in the lower right-hand corner.

The figure-eight-shaped polygon is different from all the other objects because its lines intersect.

73

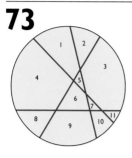

The illustration above shows four cuts dividing a cake into eleven pieces. As a general rule, try to place each new cut across all the previous cuts. In that way every *n*th cut creates *n* new pieces.

Lines	Pieces	Total
0	1	1
1	1 + 1	2
2	2 + 2	4
3	4 + 3	7
4	7 + 4	11
5	11 + 5	16

and so on

The general principle can be written as a general formula for *n* number of cuts:
$(n(n+1))/2 + 1$.

74

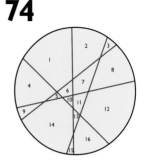

If you understand the general rule (see previous puzzle), this should be easy: if four cuts can make eleven pieces, then a fifth cut across the previous four will make five new pieces, for a total of sixteen.

75

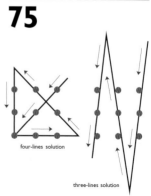

four-lines solution

three-lines solution

76 Once gained, a valuable insight can be generalized. If you have solved the problem of the nine points, the answer to problems involving greater numbers of points should come easily. For this problem five lines are needed.

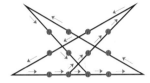

77 In general, the number of compartments crossed by the laser equals the sum of the two sides of the box minus the greatest common divisor of those two numbers. In this instance:

$$10 + 14 - 2 = 22.$$

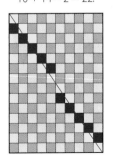

78

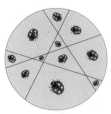

79 Since Fido is tied to a tree, he can reach anywhere within a ten-foot radius of the tree. His bowl is five feet from the tree, on the opposite side from where Fido started.

80

Most people think that three is the best answer. But if the three trees surround a steep hill or valley, then a fourth tree can be planted at the top of the hill or at the bottom of the valley, forming a tetrahedron. A tetrahedron is a three-dimensional shape made of four equilateral triangles, and therefore all four of its points are equidistant.

81

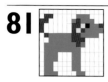

82

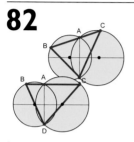

Begin by creating a triangle that connects points B and C to point D. You will find as you move points B and C around—careful to make sure that line BC always runs through point A—that the angles BDC, DBC and BCD remain the same. That means that the way to make line BAC the longest is by making lines BD and CD the longest they can be. Lines BD and CD are at their longest when they are the diameters of their respective circles. It is then that line BAC is at its longest.

It just so happens that when *BD* and *CD* run through the diameters of the circles, line *BAC* is perpendicular to line *AD*.

83

Two solutions are possible. The hidden snake is either green or blue.

84

This is another example of a problem concerning lines, intersections and restrictions on possible configurations. With *n* lines, a maximum of (n (n − 1))/2 intersections is possible. Fewer intersections are also possible, down to (n − 1) intersections, a case in which all but one of the lines run parallel.

85 There are exactly eight two-distance sets; all eight are illustrated here. In each figure the red lines have one length, and the blue lines have another.

86

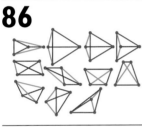

87

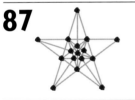

88

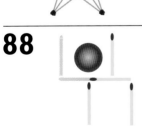

89

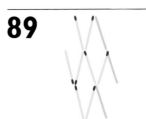

90 With four matchsticks five configurations are possible. With five matchsticks there are twelve possible configurations.

91

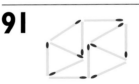

The solution shown here requires twelve matches meeting at eight points in the plane. A triangular pyramid with six matches meeting at four points would do it in space.

92

93 The linkage illustrated below is a schematic representation of the famous Watt's linkage, which draws a figure-eight-shaped curve. Part of that curve—called Bernoulli's lemniscate—is a nearly straight line.

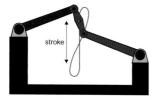

stroke

94 The path is approximately a straight line.

CHAPTER 4 SOLUTIONS

95 The only way to get to the ladybug's friend is through the red flower at the top of the diagram, so red must represent up.

Purple cannot be up, and if it were down, the ladybug's first move would be off the diagram. If purple meant left, then the ladybug would move to a yellow flower and the only allowable direction for pink would be right—a never-ending loop! So purple must represent right.

After figuring out that, it is easy to tell that blue represents left and yellow represents down.

96 A pirate with one peg leg pushed a two-wheeled cart. The pirate's dog walked beside him.

97

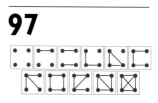

98 When he solved the Seven Bridges of Königsberg problem, Leonhard Euler discovered the general rule for tackling this class of puzzle. The secret is to count the number of paths leading from each point of intersection, or junction. If more than two junctions possess an odd number of paths, the pattern is impossible to trace.

In this instance, paths 4 and 5 are impossible.

If there are exactly two junctions that have an odd number of paths, the problem may be solved, but only if you begin and end at those two junctions. Path 7 has this property; to fully trace it, you must start at one of the lower corners and finish at the other.

99 The Hamilton Circuit:
1-5-6-2-8-4-10-11-9-3-7-1

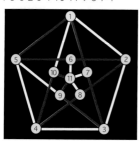

100 There are ten allowable routes.

101

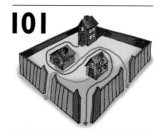

102 You can trace the figure, but only if you start at one of the blue points and end at the other.

103 The worm can crawl 22 centimeters, as shown below.

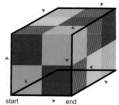

start   end

104 Puzzle master Sam Loyd first published his Mars puzzle in *Our Puzzle Magazine* in 1907; ten thousand readers wrote in saying they had tried to solve the problem and found "there is no possible way." Those ten thousand readers had solved the puzzle—THERE IS NO POSSIBLE WAY.

107

105

108

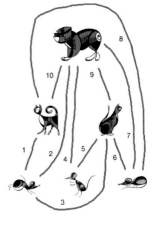

106

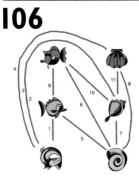

109

The four arrows in each row and column point in a different direction.

112

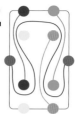

110

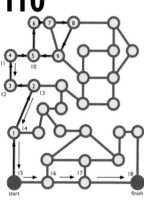

113

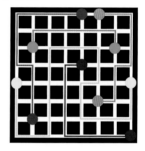

111

Circuit board #3 is the right one.

114

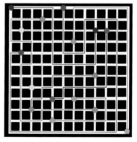

115 Before taking into account the symmetries of the cube, you can place the arrows in 4,096 (4^6) different ways. But eliminating configurations that are symmetrical duplicates leaves you with just 192 different ways to label the cube with arrows.

116 Line number 5 can be moved so that it crosses only one other line. That makes for nine intersections, which is the fewest possible when interconnecting seven different points.

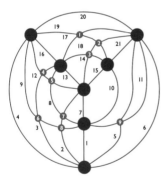

117

118 The sixteen tree graphs that connect the four points are illustrated below.

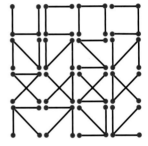

119 One solution is shown. There are many others, but all will have eighteen branches.

In the case of strings and beads, the correct answer can be suspended in the manner shown, and each bead will hang from exactly one piece of string. Therefore, the number of strings or lines or branches is equal to the number of beads or points, minus one.

No matter how you draw your tree, that is both the maximum and the minimum number of lines.

122 The path formed when one object chases another object that moves in a predetermined way has a special name: the pursuit curve, or tractrix.

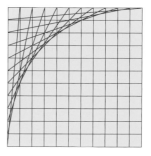

120 Each row and column contains arrows that point in the eight main directions.

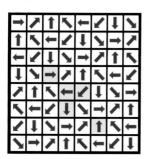

121 The route is 5, 1, 2, 4, 3

123 1. Round manhole covers cannot fall through their round holes accidentally. Square or other polygonal covers can.

2. Heavy round covers can be rolled into position, while other shapes would have to be carried.

3. Round covers can cover holes no matter how they are oriented vis-à-vis the hole. Square covers fit only when they are positioned in one of four orientations.

124 As the rollers are moved forward, their point of contact with the weight moves backward at a rate of 1 meter a turn. But the rollers are also in contact with the ground and moving forward in comparison with it at a rate of 1 meter a turn. Together, that means that the weight moves forward in relation to the ground at a rate of 2 meters per full turn.

125 The combined areas of the two red crescents—which are the areas of the two small semicircles not covered by the large black semicircle—equal the area of the right triangle itself.

Although the circle itself cannot be squared, other figures bounded by circular arcs can be. That fact arouses false hope in those who would still like to square the circle.

126 The area of the red parts is slightly more than 1.3 times greater than that of the black areas. The black areas seem larger because of an optical illusion.

127

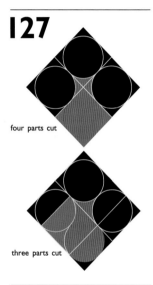

four parts cut

three parts cut

128 The bigger circle has twice the area of the smaller one. Simply put, a diagonal running from the center of the square is equal to the square root of two times the distance from the center of the square to the middle of one side. That diagonal is the radius for the large square; the distance to the middle of a side is the radius of the other. Since the area of a circle is proportional to the square of the radius, the larger circle has twice the area of the smaller one.

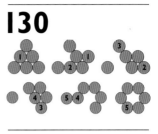

130

131

129 The area of the sickle is equal to the area of a circle that has a diameter of L.

The famous Greek scientist Archimedes first solved this problem, which now bears his name.

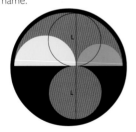

132

There are basically five ways to arrange two circles on a plane.

There are ten common tangents, as illustrated at right.

Yes. If the circles were identical, cases 4 and 5 would not be possible.

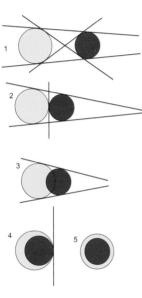

133

The three yellow circles will grow so large that they become, in the limit, the sides of a triangle. The red circle will become an inscribed circle in that triangle.

134

There are twelve polygons possible with these five points. Only two of the polygons are regular; the rest can be divided into two groups—essentially, two shapes in five different orientations each.

135

The color of the circle depends upon the number of circles it touches.

136 One of many solutions.

139 Six identical circles, as shown.

137

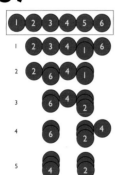

138 Every triangle has this property. The nine-point circle is half the size of the circumcircle (the circle that passes through all three vertices of the triangle), and its center is halfway between the center of the circumcenter and the orthocenter.

140 Red circle's diameter = $\frac{1}{2}$ Yellow circle's diameter = $\frac{1}{4}$

Green circle's diameter = $\frac{1}{4}$ $(2 - \sqrt{2})$, or about $\frac{1}{6}$

141 The three intersections of the tangent lines will always lie on a straight line. Imagine that the circles are three spheres of unequal size upon a flat plane. The lines between the circles are lines of perspective, which converge on the horizon.

142 Because of the great size of the sphere, there is quite a bit of safe space where the wall of the tunnel meets the floor. If he squeezes himself into that space, he can let the stone roll past him and escape.

143 The optimal solution is

Turn 1: 1, 2, 3, 4, 5
Turn 2: 2, 3, 4, 5, 6
Turn 3: 2, 3, 4, 5, 7

144 One coin rolling over another rotates twice as much as one might have anticipated. In this instance the coin rolls through two full circumferences (a third of a circumference for each coin), so it makes four revolutions.

And it will once again face left.

145 Curiously enough, the point will trace a straight line—the diameter of the larger circle.

146 The plane is 50 kilometers from the North Pole. During its eastbound leg, the plane remained a constant distance from the pole.

147 The volume of the cylinder is exactly equal to the volume of the sphere plus the volume of the cone. This is a fundamental theorem on which the determination of the volume of the sphere depended. Archimedes considered it one of his greatest triumphs.

The ratio of a cone, sphere and cylinder of the same height and radius is quite elegant:

1:2:3

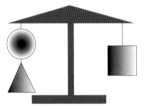

148 The intuitive answer is that since 2 meters is inconsequential compared to the circumference of the Earth, the belt would hardly budge. But in this case intuition is wrong.

A little analysis shows why. The circumference of the Earth is 2π times its radius, and the length of the belt is 2π times both the radius of the Earth and the height that the belt is pulled off the surface. If the difference between those two lengths is 2 meters, then:

$2\pi(r + x) - 2\pi r = 2$ meters

$2\pi r + 2\pi x - 2\pi r =$

$2\pi x = 2$ meters

$x = 1/\pi$ meters, or about .33 meters

The same answer would hold for an "Earth" of any size, even one the size of a tennis ball.

149 The shortest path—the straight line—is not the quickest. Instead, the ball that rolls on the cycloidal track will be the first to arrive. Amazingly, the cycloidal path is the longest of the four.

The cycloid is called the curve of quickest descent, or brachitochrone. The ball descending the cycloid reaches a high speed early in its descent and uses that speed to race ahead of the others.

150 Imagine that the four cuts have created a tetrahedron in the interior of the sphere. Based on that tetrahedron, the sphere has been divided into the following regions: four at the vertices, six

at the edges, four at the faces of the tetrahedron, and the tetrahedron itself. The total is fifteen regions.

151 Imagine that you can split the cylinder and lay it flat, as shown. According to the Pythagorean theorem:

$c^2 = a^2 + b^2 = 9 + 16 = 25$ meters

$c = 5$ meters

Thus, length of the rope is 4×5 meters, or 20 meters.

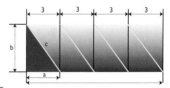

152 The area of the cycloid is three times that of the generating circle. That answer shocked mathematicians when it was first discovered.

The length of the cycloid arch, from cusp to cusp, is four times the diameter of the circle, which was also an unexpected result. Mathematicians were certain that it would be an irrational number, much like the circumference of the circle. As a curve, the cycloid is much more complex than the circle, so it is little wonder that the discovery that its length is so simple would be surprising.

153 The sphere and the cylinder have the same surface area: $4\pi r^2$.

154 1. A cut parallel to the base makes a circle.

2. A cut parallel to a line generating the cone makes a parabola.

3. A cut inclined to the axis at an angle greater than the semivertical of the cone makes an ellipse.

4. A cut inclined to the axis at an angle less than the semivertical of the cone makes a hyperbola.

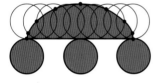

155 The problem lies in drawing the swords from the scabbards. It is impossible for the warrior with the wavy sword to pull it out of its scabbard. The other swords will go in and out of their scabbards, although the helical sword must be "unscrewed," a time-consuming act that would leave its owner at a bit of a disadvantage.

CHAPTER 6 SOLUTIONS

156 The pink shape is the only polygon shown that is not regular; not all of its sides and angles are identical.

157

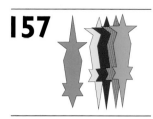

158
The result will always be 1. The operation you worked out,

points − sides + regions = 1

is Euler's formula. It is an important mathematical relationship and a beautiful example of simplicity amid complexity.

159
The missing number is 5. The sum of the numbers on the convex angles of each polygon is five times greater than the sum of the numbers on the concave angles.

160
The key to understanding this problem is realizing that for a rectangle divided by a diagonal, the area on one side of the diagonal is equal to that of the other side. For a one-by-two rectangle, that means each side has an area of 1 square unit. There are nine squares divided in this way; that means 4.5 square units are enclosed by the band and 4.5 are outside the band. Add the 4.5 to the three squares completely enclosed by the band to get the total area, which is 7.5 units squared.

161
The first step to solving the puzzle is turning the inner hexagon so that its corners touch the outer hexagon. Then divide the inner hexagon into six equilateral triangles, and each of those equilateral triangles into three identical isosceles triangles. It is clear that the six areas of the outer hexagon uncovered by the inner hexagon are equal in size to those isosceles triangles. From that, it is easy to see that the outer hexagon has an area of 4 square units.

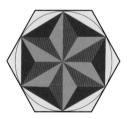

162 Four points are not enough—imagine a triangle with an interior point. It takes five points to guarantee a convex quadrilateral. This fact was demonstrated by the Erdös-Szekeres theorem in 1935. If you surround the five points with a rubber band, there are three possible outcomes:

1. The band forms a convex quadrilateral with the fifth point tucked inside.

2. The band forms a pentagon; connecting two of the vertices will result in a convex quadrilateral.

3. The band forms a triangle with two points inside. Connect the two interior points with a line—on one side of the line, there will be one vertex of the triangle; on the other side, two vertices. Connect those two vertices to the interior points to make a convex quadrilateral.

163 There are exactly fifteen identical overlapping equilateral triangles. If you counted the triangles formed by the overlap, there would be a total of twenty-eight.

164 Both areas are identical. The total area of the small triangles is equal to that of the big triangle. And the overlapping parts in white decrease both equally.

165 Yes. This mysterious and completely unexpected fact was discovered by English mathematician Frank Morley in 1899—which is why it's called Morley's triangle.

166 There are twenty-seven triangles.
In general, the number of triangles of different sizes in a triangular grid follows the sequence 1, 5, 13, 27, 48, 78, 118, etc., for triangles of increasing size. For triangles with an even number of levels, the general formula is

$$\frac{n(n + 2)(2n + 1)}{8}$$

For odd numbers of levels, the general formula is

$$\frac{n(n + 2)(2n + 1) - 1}{8}$$

167

168

169

To enclose the most area, the panels should be opened at 135 degrees. The area is one-quarter of a regular octagon.

170
The area of the triangle to the area of the hexagon is 2:3.

171

172

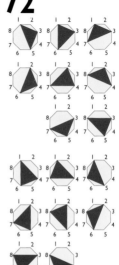

173

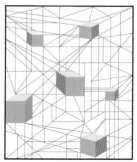

174 It takes just one cut, as shown. Join the triangle created by the cut to the other end of the parallelogram to form the rectangle.

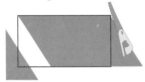

175 In general, a convex polygon of n sides needs $n - 3$ diagonals to triangulate it, and those diagonals create $n - 2$ triangles. Thus, for the heptagon, four diagonals make five triangles; the nonagon needs six diagonals to make seven triangles; the undecagon employs eight diagonals to make nine triangles.

176

177 simple solution would be walls that form a polygon of fourteen sides. Another solution, one requiring the least amount of floor area, would be to make the walls form a seven-pointed star.

revolving security camera

178

area (T) = area (JLNM) – area (JKM) – area (KLN) = $(a + b)(2a + 2b)/2 - ab - ab = a^2 + b^2 = EB^2 = $ area (S)

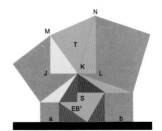

179

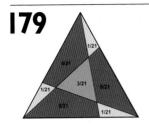

Each trisecting line divides the triangle into $1/3$ or $7/21$, which is again divided into three parts, which simple observation tells us can be only $1/21$, $5/21$ and $1/21$. It follows that the central triangle is $3/21$.

---

180 To create a triangle from three strips, it is necessary that the sum of the lengths of any two sides be greater than the length of the third side. The green and blue sets of strips do not follow this rule and thus cannot form triangles.

---

181 Four cameras are sufficient (see the red dots in the diagram). There are many ways to arrange them.

182

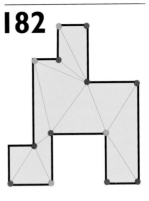

The three blue points are the solution.

---

183 This will work with every triangle.
In the example shown, the triangles are constructed inward; as you can see, the centers still form an equilateral triangle that has the same center as the original triangle. Interestingly, the difference in the area of the three constructed triangles is equal to the area of the original triangle.

184

No. The divisions of Cake 1 and Cake 3 are equal, but the red group gets bigger slices from Cake 2.

If the number of chords (or cuts through the cake) is even and equal to four or more, the areas (or pieces of cake) are always equal.

If the number of chords is odd or less than four, the areas will not be equal—unless the chords go through the center of the circle, as they do in Cake 1.

This puzzle was inspired by the "Pizza Problem," which was discovered by L. J. Upton in 1968, and proved by Larry Carter and Stan Wagon in 1994.

185

The order is yellow, orange, red, pink, violet, light green, dark green, light blue, dark blue and lime. The order is also that of an increasing number of sides, from the triangle with three to the dodecagon with twelve.

186

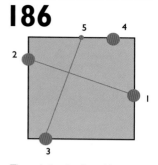

The solution begins with drawing a line between two points, such as the one between points 1 and 2. Then draw a line from point 3 that is both equal in length and perpendicular to the line between 1 and 2. The endpoint of that line, marked as 5, is obviously on the line of the square.

Draw a line through points 4 and 5, and draw a parallel line through point 3. To complete the square, draw lines perpendicular to these lines through points 1 and 2. The four lines will intersect to form a square.

187

Twenty-one squares are possible.

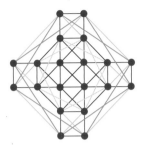

188

You can make three actual words. The first letter can be any one of the three; the second can be either of the two remaining letters; the third is the letter left over:
$3 \times 2 \times 1 = 6$ possible words. The possibilities are

OWN, ONW, NOW, NWO, WON, WNO.

For n different letters, numbers or objects, the number of possible arrangements can be calculated:

$$n \times (n - 1) \times (n - 2) \times \ldots$$
$$3 \times 2 \times 1$$

This number is called n factorial and is abbreviated as n!.

189

With four children per group, there are six different permutations in which every girl sits next to another girl, as shown. There is also the possible arrangement of four boys and no girls.

190

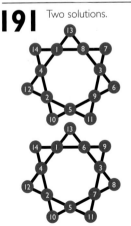

191

Two solutions.

192 There are just six different arrangements for the three objects. There are three different possibilities for the leftmost fruit. For each fruit, there are two different possibilities for what goes in the middle; and for each left and middle, there is just one possibility for what goes on the right.

$$3 \times 2 \times 1 = 6$$

The operation from one arrangement to another is called a permutation.

193 There are 16 possible pairs.

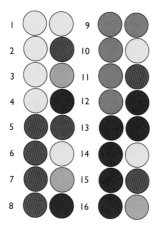

194 In 5,040 different ways.

195

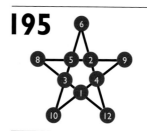

196

Mathematicians call this a universal cycle for 2-sequences. It exists for any number of colors or objects; the cycle is the square of the number of colors.

197 One of many ways.

198

202

199

203

200

201 There are two solutions, shown below. In Dürer's "diabolic" magic squares, there are many sets of numbers that add up to the magic constant. Look, for instance, at the two-by-two square in the top left-hand corner: 16, 3, 5 and 10 add up to 34.

204

One of many solutions is shown. This one was obtained by taking the "Magic Square of Dürer" (PlayThink 201) and subtracting 17 from every value greater than 8.

205

The sum of all nine digits is 45; distributed across three rows or columns, that means the "magic constant" is 15.

In general, the constant for magic squares with any number of rows and columns can be found without adding the digits. For any number of rows n, the magic constant is

$$(n^3 + n)/2$$

To solve the Lo-Shu, you should first realize that there are eight possible triads of digits that add up to 15:

9-5-1; 9-4-2; 8-6-1; 8-5-2; 8-4-3; 7-6-2; 7-5-3; 6-5-4

The digit in the center of the square appears in four lines (a column, a row and both horizontals). Since 5 is the only digit that appears in four triads, it must be the center digit. Since 9 appears in only two triads, it must go into the middle of a row or column, which is completed with 1 to make the 9-5-1 triad. Similarly, 3 and 7 are in only two triads, so they must be in the

middle of a row or column. The remaining four numbers can fit in only one way—an elegant proof of the uniqueness of the Lo-Shu solution.

206

Only the flipped hinges are shown.

207

There are fifteen different combinations. For each monkey you could choose any of the three donkeys, so there are three possible pairs. Since this is true with each of the five monkeys, that leads to fifteen possible pairs.

208

209

Here are two of an infinite number of solutions.

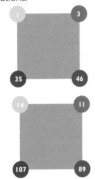

212

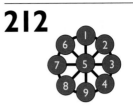

213

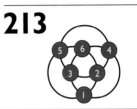

214

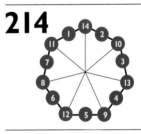

210

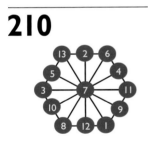

211

n = 5;
k = 11;

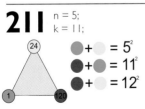

$+$ $=5^2$
$+$ $=11^2$
$+$ $=12^2$

215

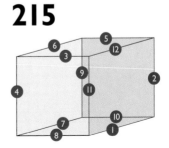

216

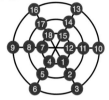

218

	↓	↘	↘	↓	↙	
↘	3	2	1	2	2	↙
↗	2	1	3	1	4	↖
↘	2	4	2	5	2	←
↘	4	2	5	2	3	←
→	3	4	2	3	3	↖
	↗	↑	↑	↗	↑	

217 Two solutions.

219

The sum of all nineteen numbers is 190, which is divisible by 5, and there are five parallel rows in each direction. Thus, the magic constant is 190 divided by 5, or 38.

In general, it is possible to arrange a set of positive integers from 1 to *n* in a hexagonal honeycomb array of *n* cells so that every straight row has a constant sum—that is, a magic constant.

As we see illustrated below, an order 3 magic hexagon is possible. But an order 2 hexagon, one that has seven cells, is impossible. The sum of the numbers from one to seven is 28, and 28 divided by three (the number of rows in each direction) is not an integer.

Likewise, magic hexagons of order 4 and order 5 are also impossible. In fact, an extremely complicated proof has shown that no magic hexagon of a size greater than order 3 is possible. What is even more astonishing is that the magic hexagon shown above, which was discovered in 1910, is the only possible solution.

220 The arrows show the motion of the squares in each pattern. The missing pattern from each sequence is shown in red.

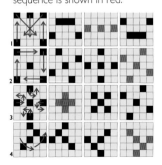

221 The yellow dot stands for the pineapple; the red dot, for the apple. There are nine different ways to distribute them among the three bowls, as shown.

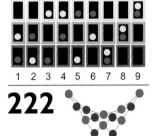

1 2 3 4 5 6 7 8 9

222

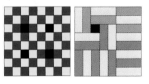

223 It is possible, but only if the monomino covers one of the squares, shown in black.

CHAPTER 8 SOLUTIONS

224

225

226

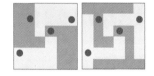

227

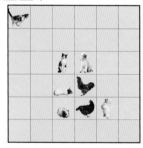

228

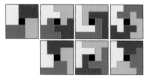

229

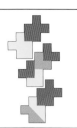

230

231

232

233

234

235

236

237

238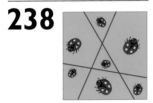

239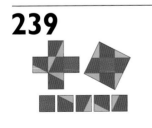

240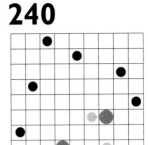

241 You can make the two squares from four pieces: one for the smaller square and three for the larger one.

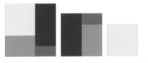

242 The task requires only seven cuts.

243

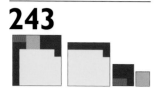

244

The pieces form a chain—when they are swung in one direction, they form an equilateral triangle; when they are swung in the opposite direction, they form a square.

The inventor of this gem of recreational mathematics was Henry Ernest Dudeney, England's most accomplished puzzle maker. Born in 1857, Dudeney was extremely successful with dissections and set many records. This dissection, however, is his most famous discovery.

245

Nine small figures, as shown.

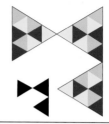

246

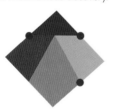

247

It takes eleven smaller triangles to completely cover the eleven-by-eleven triangle. One solution is shown.

248

The maximum number of holes that can be made on a board cannot exceed the number of dominoes. In fact, if the length of one side of the board is evenly divisible by three, then the maximum number of holes is the product of the two sides, divided by three.

249

250

251

252

253
The uncovered square can be anywhere on the board. Three sample arrangements are shown below; through reflection and rotation, one of the arrangements will uncover any given square.

254
In the first and third examples, about three-quarters of the triangle is covered. In the other two, much less is covered.

255
The large replica holds sixteen smaller T-tiles.

256 One of the most counterintuitive facts in geometry is that only three regular polygons—the equilateral triangle, the square and the regular hexagon—are capable of tessellating a plane.

There is a beautiful logic behind the rarity of regular tessellations. At every point in which the vertices of the tessellating polygons meet, the sum of the angles of those vertices must equal 360 degrees. The only regular polygons that can tessellate, then, are the ones whose angles are factors of 360.

Six equilateral triangles, each with angles of 60 degrees, can meet at a point—and so they can tessellate.

Four squares, each with angles of 90 degrees, can meet at a point—and so squares can tessellate.

Pentagons have internal angles of 108 degrees—not a factor of 360—and so pentagons cannot tessellate.

Three hexagons, each with angles of 120 degrees, can meet at a point, and so hexagons can tessellate.

As you can see, the next whole number that can meet at a point is 2—making for 180 degrees on each side. That's not a tessellation—it is a bisection. Therefore, only an equilateral triangle, a square and a regular hexagon are capable of tessellating a plane.

257 The twelve different ways of joining five identical squares are shown above. Such shapes are called pentominoes.

258

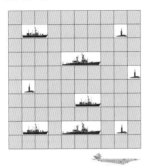

CHAPTER 9 SOLUTIONS

259 Each successive ring has $6(n - 1)$ elements. That means the next hexagonal number is $37 + 6(5 - 1) = 61$.

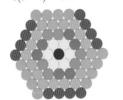

260 Squares are formed by the sum of the series of odd numbers, beginning with 1.

$1^2 = 1$
$2^2 = 1 + 3 = 4$
$3^2 = 1 + 3 + 5 = 9$
$4^2 = 1 + 3 + 5 + 7 = 16$
and so on

The seventh square would be $7^2 = 1 + 3 + 5 + 7 + 9 + 11 + 13 = 49$.

261 The tetrahedral series can be expressed by the formula $n(n + 1)(n + 2)/6$. That gives a series 1, 4, 10, 20, 35, 56, 84 ...

The square pyramidal series can be expressed in the formula $n(n+1)(2n+1)/6$. That gives a sequence of 1, 5, 14, 30, 55, 91, 140 ...

262

$$12 = 9 + 1 + 1 + 1$$

$$15 = 9 + 4 + 1 + 1$$

263 Gauss realized that the series 1 + 2 + 3 + 4 ... 97 + 98 + 99 + 100 could be written as:

1 + 100 + 2 + 99 + 3 + 98 + 4 + 97 ...

or 101 times 50, to get the total, 5,050.

This trick works for any sum of sequential integers. Indeed, the general formula is simply $n(n + 1)/2$, which is the equation for triangular numbers.

264 Just five. The same pickers who can pick five apples in five seconds can pick sixty apples in sixty seconds; they average an apple a second.

265 The unique solution for four pairs of blocks is shown here.

The Scottish mathematician C. Dudley Langford first laid out the general form of this problem in the 1950s after watching his son play with colored blocks. It turns out that the problem has a solution only if the number of pairs of blocks is a multiple of 4, or is 1 less than a multiple of 4.

266 Since there are seven pages before page 8, there must be seven pages after page 21. The newspaper has twenty-eight pages.

267 There are many examples: 243 + 675 = 918; 341 + 586 = 927; 154 + 782 = 936; 317 + 628 = 945; 216 + 738 = 954 ... and so on.

268 Twenty ladybugs.

269 Swap the 8 and the 9, then turn the 9 upside-down so it reads as a 6. Both columns will then total 18.

270 One of many possible solutions.

271

272

273 The ten digits can be permutated in 10!, or 3,628,800, ways. But since all the ways that start with 0 must be dropped, the actual number is 362,880 lower, for a total of 3,265,920.

274 Each number is the sum of its neighbors immediately above, to the left and to the upper left diagonal. Following this rule, the missing number is 63.

275

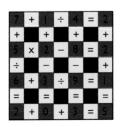

276

$$2,520 = 5 \times 7 \times 8 \times 9$$

277 The answer is 20 years old because 210 is the twentieth triangular number, equal to the sum of all the numbers from 1 to 20.

278 The next four numbers are 21, 34, 55 and 89.

Each number is the sum of the two numbers preceding it. As the sequence continues, the ratio of successive terms approaches the famous golden ratio, 1:1.6180037

279 Each term is a description of the number preceding it: "11" means there's one 1; "21" means there are two 1s; "1211" means there is one 2 and one 1; "111221" means there is one 1, one 2 and two 1s.

312211

280 The numbers double as they run from left to right horizontally; the numbers go up by 2 as they run from top to bottom diagonally.

281 The numbers make up the cake-cutting sequence—the maximum number of pieces that can be made from a given number of straight cuts through a plane. As a general rule, each *n*th cut will make *n* number of new pieces. Thus, for the sixth cut, the number of pieces will be 16 + 6, or 22.

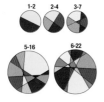

282 The sequence is based on the principle of persistence, in which the digits of a number are multiplied together to get another number; the function is carried out until only a one-digit number remains.

Thus, the last number in the sequence is 8.

283 The possible answers are 52 and 25, 63 and 36, 74 and 47, 85 and 58, or 96 and 69. But the ages that match up with how long my friend has been practicing magic are 74 and 47.

284 IOTOIO

285

$17 \times 4 = 68 + 25 = 93$

$$\times \begin{array}{c} \boxed{1}\,\boxed{7} \\ \boxed{4} \end{array}$$

$= \boxed{6}\,\boxed{8} + \boxed{2}\,\boxed{5} = \boxed{9}\,\boxed{3}$

286

287 The puzzle begins with one hundred separate pieces and ends with one complete cluster. Since each move reduces the number of pieces or clusters by one, only ninety-nine moves are needed.

288 Add 40 to both.

170	30
+40	+40
210	70

$$\frac{Y}{Z} = \frac{210}{70} \quad \boxed{X=40}$$

289 $2^6 - 63 = 1$

290

4	1	4	2	5	2
1		1	5		5
4	1	4	2	5	2
	7	1	0	9	0
7		7	9		9
1	7	1	0	9	0

291 Yes, there *is* enough information to work this out. If there are even two red flowers, then it will be possible to pick a pair without one being purple. So there is only one red flower, and the rest are purple.

292 There can't be even two red flowers, or else it will be possible to pick two reds and a yellow and not have any purple flowers out of three. Similar logic dictates that there can't be more than one purple or one yellow flower. Therefore, there are only three flowers in the entire garden.

293 There were twenty-three emus and twelve camels.

294 I saw twenty-two two-legged birds and fourteen four-legged beasts.

295 To solve this problem, you have to work out the number of possible pairs for the nine friends. For any given friend, four separate dinners are necessary to see all eight cohorts.

Day 1—Kate, David, Lucy
Day 2—Emily, Jane, Theo
Day 3—Mary, James, John
Day 4—Kate, Emily, Mary
Day 5—David, Jane, James
Day 6—Lucy, Theo, John
Day 7—Kate, Jane, John
Day 8—Lucy, Jane, Mary
Day 9—David, Theo, Mary
Day 10—Lucy, Emily, James
Day 11—Kate, Theo, James
Day 12—David, Emily, John

296 Since the mother cat has two lives left, the kittens must divide up the remaining twenty-three. That means there are two possible answers: seven kittens (one has five lives left and six have three lives) or five kittens (one with three lives and four with five lives).

297

Day 1—4-5-2	7-1-9	6-8-3
Day 2—7-8-5	4-3-1	6-9-2
Day 3—8-1-2	4-7-6	9-3-5
Day 4—1-5-7	3-2-8	9-4-6
Day 5—8-4-1	5-6-2	3-7-9
Day 6—7-2-4	8-9-5	1-6-3

298

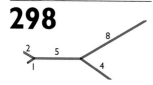

299 Minimal length rulers, invented by Solomon W. Golomb, can only be "perfect" up to length 6. All higher length rulers are "imperfect," since some distances occur more than once or don't occur at all. Using an 11-unit ruler, it is impossible to place the markers so that a 6-unit distance is measured.

300 There were fifteen ladybugs:

$$3 + 5 + 6 + 1 = 15$$

301

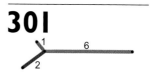

302 The red triangles occupy an area that is roughly one-third that of the square.

303 The red arm occupies exactly one-fourth of the square. You can divide the entire square into four such spiral arms.

304 Sallows found this eight-sided golygon to be the simplest possible; it has the interesting ability to tessellate in the plane. The next simplest golygon has sixteen sides; there are twenty-eight variations of it. Martin Gardner proved that the number of sides in a golygon must be a multiple of 8.

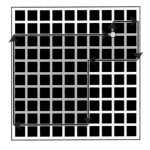

305 Although many properties of primes remain unproven, one famous proof has demonstrated that there is always a prime between every integer greater than 1 and that integer's double.

306 None of the 362,880 numbers will be prime.

In each case the sum of their digits is 45, which is divisible by 9. And any number that has digits adding up to a multiple of 9 is itself a multiple of 9. This simple divisibility check shows why none of the numbers can be prime.

307 The stack of images would approach a height twice that of the original picture, but it would never actually reach that point. The sum of $1 + \frac{1}{2} + \frac{1}{4} + \frac{1}{8} + \frac{1}{16} \ldots$ is less than 2.

308 Examine the sum of the divisors of 284:
$1 + 2 + 4 + 5 + 10 + 11 + 20 + 22 + 44 + 55 + 110 = 284$
Now look at the divisors for 220:
$1 + 2 + 4 + 71 + 142 = 220$
If the sum of the divisors of a number is equal to a number whose divisors are equal to the first, the pair is said to be amicable. The smallest known pair is 220 and 284.

309 The complete decomposition of 420 is $42 \times 10 = 6 \times 7 \times 2 \times 5 = 2 \times 3 \times 7 \times 2 \times 5$.

310

Anne's neighbors can be either two boys or two girls. If they are girls, then each of them must be neighbored by another girl, since they are both next to Anne. So in the instance where Anne's neighbors are girls, the entire circle must be girls.

Since there are boys in the circle, the circle is obviously not all girls. That means Anne's neighbors must both be boys, each of whom is neighbored by Anne and another girl. This alternating pattern continues around the circle, so that the circle contains twelve boys and twelve girls.

311

$1 + 2 + 3 = 1 \times 2 \times 3 = 6$

312

The answer is 24, composed of 1, 2, 3, 4, 6, 8, 12 and 24.

313

Before you turn your back, you check to see how many coins are showing heads. You know that the number of heads will increase by two, decrease by two or stay the same for every pair of coins that is turned over. Therefore, if the initial number of heads is odd, the number will remain odd, no matter how many pairs of coins are turned.

When you turn back around, you count the number of heads that are now showing. If the number is odd, as at the start (or even, as at the start), the covered coin must be a tail. If the number of heads is even for an odd start (or odd for an even start), the covered coin must be a head.

This simple trick helps demonstrate the importance of parity: the odd-even parity of this system is preserved as long as pairs of coins (not individual coins) are turned over.

314

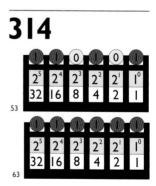

315 The thief will always stay one step ahead unless the policeman moves first and changes the parity of the game. He can do that by going around the triangular block just once, catching the thief in seven or fewer moves.

316

317

318 Try as they might, they will fail. That is because turning over two glasses at a time changes the number of upright glasses by two or by zero. And although the number of upright glasses in the first setup was one, so that adding two gave you a total of three, the number of upright glasses in the second setup is zero. Changing two at a time will allow your friends to fluctuate between zero glasses and two glasses, but they will never get to three glasses. In other words, the first setup has an odd parity, while the second

setup has an even parity. In both instances, turning over two glasses at a time will not change that parity.

319

320 Many people claim that there is not enough information provided to solve this problem. But that is because they have taken too narrow a view.

The key is understanding what a lightbulb does: it produces not only light but heat, and it remains warm many minutes after it has been switched off.

With that in mind, you can find the solution fairly easily. First, turn on switch 1 and leave it on for several minutes so that the bulb will get good and hot. Next, turn off switch 1 and turn on switch 2, and then go quickly to the attic. If the light is on, then switch 2 works the lamp; if the bulb is dark but warm, switch 1 works the lamp. If the bulb is both dark and cold, switch 3—the one that has not been used—works the lamp.

321 Such a bet is a losing proposition. Only three out of six possible random settings allow for the light to be turned on with the flip of just one switch.

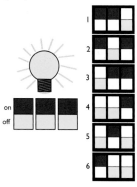

324

The missing necklace.

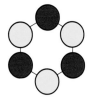

322 There are three different necklaces possible. The different necklaces can be described by the number of red beads between the green ones: either none, one, or two.

323 The parity of the initial setup is odd, and an even number of moves will not change that. Therefore, both all-upright and all-inverted conclusions are impossible.

325 This solution is the only one possible. Longer binary wheels are used to code messages in telephone transmission and radar mapping. University of California–Davis mathematician Sherman K. Stein called such binary structures memory wheels; they have also been called Ouroborean rings, a name derived from the mythological snake that ate its tail.

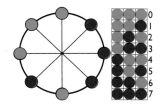

326

There are at least two solutions:
1-1-1-1-0-0-0-0-1-1-0-1-0-0-1-0 and 1-1-1-1-0-0-0-0-1-1-0-0-1-1-0-1-0.

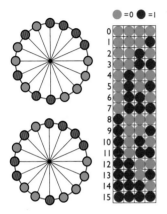

● =0 ● =1

0
1
2
3
4
5
6
7
8
9
10
11
12
13
14
15

327

You have to attack problems like this one in a systematic fashion, or the complexities will boggle your mind. The best way to visualize the variables is to draw a cell chart with, say, the positions across the top and the names down the side. Put an X in a cell that has been logically ruled out, and put a * in a cell you believe is correct.

	CHAIRMAN	DIRECTOR	SECRETARY
Gerry	X	•	X
Anita	X	X	*
Rose	*	X	X

Then work your way through the premises:

Gerry has a brother, and the secretary is an only child, so Gerry can't be the secretary.

Rose earns more than the director, and the secretary earns less than anyone, so Rose can be neither the director nor the secretary.

The conclusions, then, are that Anita is the secretary, Gerry is the director and Rose is the chairman.

328 The reflexive answer is that if boys and girls are equally likely, the probability that the other child is a girl is ½.

But the reflex is wrong. There are four possible combinations for the Smiths' two children: boy-boy, boy-girl, girl-boy and girl-girl. One possibility (boy-boy) can be ruled out, but the other three are equally likely. Of the possibilities that remain, only one involves a second girl, so the likelihood that the Smiths have a second girl is only ⅓.

This problem is an example of conditional probability—that is, the probability of one event given the fact that another event has occurred. The results are counterintuitive and generally misunderstood.

329 The question is, rather, *where* can you build it? Only on the North Pole.

330 The first three rules eliminate 118 of the 120 possible permutations of the five disks. The last rule selects one of the remaining two possibilities.

331 The clerk forgot to mention that the parrot was deaf.

332 Fish.

333 The note meant: "I ought to owe nothing for I ate nothing."

334 Green.

335 Fifty percent of the birds will be watched by one other bird, and another 25 percent will be watched by two other birds. That leaves 25 percent unwatched.

336 He married the sister first.

337 The first child says he is a truth teller. The statement is true if he's telling the truth and false if he is lying.

What the second child says is true no matter whether the first child is telling the truth. She is therefore a truth teller.

The truth of the third child's statement depends on the truthfulness of the first child. If the first child is lying, the third is telling the truth; if the first is telling the truth, the third is lying.

The possibilities are either (from left to right): liar–truth teller–truth teller or truth teller–truth teller–liar. Either way, two are telling the truth and one is lying.

338 The chances of drawing a red ball are $^{20}/_{50}$, or 40 percent. The chances of drawing a blue ball are $^{30}/_{50}$, or 60 percent.

339 You are better off fighting the brontosaurus. Although your chances of beating any stegosaur is $^1/_2$, beating three in series brings the probability to $^1/_2 \times ^1/_2 \times ^1/_2$, or $^1/_8$.

340 You should take the bet. The probability of at least one man getting his own hat back is almost .632.

341 His reasoning was wrong. Sure, the chance of an unlikely event happening twice is fairly low, but the sailor's safety can't be calculated just by looking at the random nature of another shell landing in that hole. For one thing, the destination of a shell is not entirely random—the guns are being aimed, and gunners who have success with one shot may try sending another round in the same direction. For another, each time a random phenomenon occurs, the probability of the specified event happening again is exactly the same. So even if the guns were not being aimed, the spot where the shell hit is just as likely to be hit with the next round as any other spot.

342 The probability that the underside matches the top is ⅔. If you see heads, there are three, not two, equally possible scenarios:
1. You see the head half of a head-tail coin.
2. You see one side of a double-headed coin.
3. You see the other side of a double-headed coin.

In two of the three cases, the underside matches the top.

This result is so counterintuitive that many people refuse to believe it. If you are skeptical, try experimenting with "coins" cut out of cardboard. Keep track of your results and see if your probabilities match what I've outlined above.

343 Number 1 is Jerry, who likes chicken. Number 2 is Ivan, who likes cakes. Number 3 is Jill, who likes salad. Number 4 is Anita, who likes fish.

344 Own the casino! The math of roulette and other casino games guarantees that, over time, the casino owners make far more money than they pay out. For every person who leaves the casino richer, there are many others who have lost considerable sums.

345

346 The two heirs swapped horses.

347 86.

348 There are six possible outcomes for rolling three marbles, and in four of those instances Peter wins. So his chances of winning are ⅔.

349 "Just between you and me" and "Split second timing."

350 1. The word three is misspelled.

2. The word *mistake* should be plural.

3. There are only two mistakes in the sentence, which is the third mistake.

351 If you count the letters, you will find there is 1 D, 2 I's, 3 S's, 4 C's, 5 O's, 6 V's, 7 E's and 8 R's. The secret word is DISCOVER.

352 The player with die A will, over the long run, win 55 percent of the time, as demonstrated in the chart below.

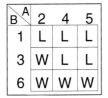

B＼A	2	4	5
1	L	L	L
3	W	L	L
6	W	W	W

353 RANGE and ANGER.

354 In the last composition the rectangle and the oval do not overlap.

355 There were fourteen squares on the sheet, six on one side and eight on the other.

356 The usual answer people give is that it should take about 100 links. But research conducted at Harvard University in Massachusetts demonstrates that any two strangers in the United States can be linked by a chain of intermediate acquaintances only five to six people long.

This problem, known as the "Small World" problem, is the basis of the popular trivia game in which one tries to link any actor to Kevin Bacon in just six steps. Both Hollywood and the world at large are examples of networks, a system with many interconnections. Chains of acquaintances have always been important, but with the revolution in travel and communication that has taken over the world in the last fifty years, people are connected through a very few steps to almost every other person on earth.

357 Only the second statement is true. Statement number 3 rules out both number 1 and number 3.

358 The passenger realized that if his face were clean, one of the other passengers would have realized that his own face was blackened by soot. Since neither of them stopped laughing, he realized his face must be sooty as well.

359 At first glance it seems the chances of a red ball remaining in the bag are 50 percent. But there are actually three—not two—equally possible states:

1. The initial red ball (A) was drawn, leaving the added red ball (C).
2. The added red ball (C) was taken, leaving the initial red ball (A).
3. The added red ball (C) was taken, leaving the blue ball (B).

As you can see, in two out of the three cases, a red ball remains in the bag.

In the initial draw, the chances of pulling out a red ball are 75 percent. But once the first ball is drawn, the odds change.

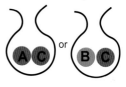

360

$$6 + 6 + 8 + 8 = 28$$
$$+ \quad + \quad + \quad +$$
$$6 + 6 + 6 + 6 = 24$$
$$+ \quad + \quad + \quad +$$
$$12 + 12 + 10 + 8 = 42$$
$$+ \quad\quad + \quad\quad + \quad\quad +$$
$$8/32 + 10/34 + 12/36 + 6/28 = 36$$

361 The chances are not $2/3$ but $1/3$. The reasoning is simple. Choose any card. Of the three remaining cards, only one is the same color, so the chances of picking it are just one in three.

Your friend's reasoning is incorrect because the three possibilities he or she considered are not equally likely.

362 The answer is ONE WORD.

363 Remarkably, the probability of two people sharing a birthday is about .5 in a group of just twenty-three people.

To calculate this, you have to look at the probability that everyone has a *different* birthday. For a group of two people, the probability is extremely high—about $\frac{364}{365}$—that they will have different birthdays. With a group of three, the probability is not as high—$\frac{363}{365}$—and since the group of three still contains the group of two, the two probabilities are multiplied. Continue along this track until the probability of everybody in the group having different birthdays drops below .5, which means the probability of two people sharing a birthday is now more than .5.

The probability approaches near certainty with ninety people or more.

364 Although Amos and Butch are sure shots, Cody's chances of survival are twice as good as the other cowboys'.

The reason is straightforward. If Amos or Butch gets the first shot, the one who gets it will eliminate the other (since they represent the greatest threat) and take his chances with Cody. Cody then has a 50 percent chance of shooting the survivor and a 50 percent chance of missing and getting shot. If Cody draws the first shot, he'd be well advised to miss, because if he actually shoots either Amos or Butch, the other could gun him down.

So Cody's chances of surviving are 50 percent.

Amos and Butch both have the same chances: If they lose the draw, they are shot in the first round; if they win the draw, one shoots the other and take his chances with Cody. Since both outcomes are equally likely, the chances for either Amos or Butch turn out to be 0 percent plus 50 percent, divided by two—or 25 percent.

365 In calculating probability, mathematicians generally limit themselves to four possible outcomes: heads-heads, tails-tails, heads-tails and tails-head. But there is can be a fifth possible result—uncountable. For example, one coin could land on edge. Or it could be lost down a grate. Or be carried off by a bird in midflight. Perhaps mathematicians should account for such occurrences when they calculate probabilities in the future.

366 In the case of our coin-flipping experiment, a surprising probability is found in Benford's law. The odds are overwhelming that at some point in a series of 200 tosses, either heads or tails will come up six or more times in a row. Most fakers don't know this and will not put such nonrandom occurrences in their fake results.

367 The formula for solving such problems has eluded mathematicians for centuries. Practical solutions are best found through simple trial and error. In the circle of thirty-six prisoners, the proper positions to plant your enemies are numbers 4, 10, 15, 20, 26 and 30.

368 There are six possible even numbers that can come up—2, 4, 6, 8, 10 and 12—and only five possible odd numbers—3, 5, 7, 9 and 11. In spite of that, as the diagram shows, there are eighteen ways to throw an even number and eighteen ways to throw an odd number. So the odds of an even number are even.

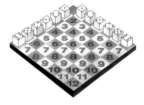

369 In any given roll of a die, the odds that a 6 will not come up are $5/6$. Since each roll of a die is independent of the others, the chances of not rolling a 6 in a given series can be calculated as:

Two rolls: $5/6 \times 5/6 = .69$
Three rolls: $5/6 \times 5/6 \times 5/6 = .57$
Four rolls: $5/6 \times 5/6 \times 5/6 \times 5/6 = .48$

which means that more often than not, you will roll at least one 6 after four rolls.

370 In the seventeenth century Antoine Gombaud Chevalier de Méré, a French nobleman with an interest in gambling, suspected that the odds were not in his favor, so he checked his suspicions with the famous mathematicians Blaise Pascal and Pierre de Fermat, who found that the probability of rolling double 6 after twenty-four throws was $\frac{35}{36}$ to the twenty-fourth power, or about .49, which meant losing in the long run.

Gombaud's small request marked the birth of the science of probability.

CHAPTER 11 SOLUTIONS

371

372 a-5, b-1, c-9

373 There are two different lengths—ten long and ten short. Each color comes in two lengths. The sequence that removes them all is short yellow, short orange, short red, short pink, short purple, short light green, short dark green, long light blue, short dark blue, long yellow, long orange, long red, long pink, long purple, long light green, long dark green, short light blue, long dark blue, short violet and long violet.

374 Only 2 and 9 are topologically identical.

375 The solution illustrates the two-color theorem.

376 Clockwise: yellow triangle, orange pentagon, red heptagon, pink nonagon, violet square, light green hexagon, blue octagon and purple decagon.

377 You will need at least three colors. One of the many possibilities is shown here.

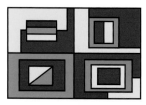

378

379 The minimum number of colors is eight, as shown.

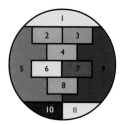

380

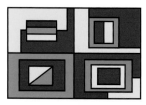

381 The capital *E* is topologically equivalent to *F, G, J, T* and *Y*.

ABCDE
FGHIJ
KLMNO
PQRST
UVWXYZ

382 The quartets are 1-9-11-14; 2-3-7-13; 4-5-6-8. That leaves the pair: 10-12.

383

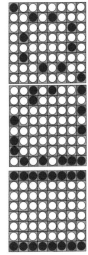

385

The unique solution is shown below.

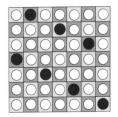

386

The diagram below shows one of the twelve different solutions, not counting rotations and reflections.

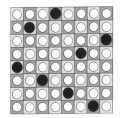

384

There is just one solution.

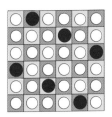

387

The illustration below shows one of four possible solutions.

388 Every shape but the pentagon can be made by slicing a cube.

389 Two disconnections, as shown, will form five lengths of one, one, three, six and twelve beads. Combining these lengths in various ways can form necklaces of one to twenty-three beads.

390 Only two of the loops will be knotted if the hose is pulled tight: the one at the bottom right and the one on the middle left.

391 With three points of intersection for the rope to overlap, there are eight different configurations for the loop. Only two of those will form a knot, as shown below. Therefore the probability is $\frac{1}{4}$.

392 The twenty-four connected cubes represent an ordinary overhand knot.

393

394

step 1

step 2   step 3

395
It turns out that it is nearly impossible to fold a sheet of newsprint in half more than eight or nine times, no matter how large or thin the sheet.

Every time you fold the sheet, you double the number of pages in the stack. One fold makes two pages, two folds make four pages; Nine folds will produce a stack of newsprint 512 pages thick—the size of a small phone book. A stack that thick prevents any additional folding.

396
It will take nineteen moves to remove the piston.

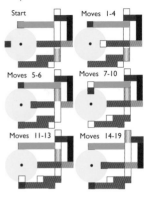

Start   Moves 1-4

Moves 5-6   Moves 7-10

Moves 11-13   Moves 14-19

397

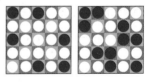

398

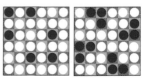

399

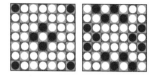

400

401
There are ten distinct ways.

402
The shortest route will not follow the edge of the cube. To envision the shortest route, imagine flattening out the faces of the cube, as shown below. If you draw a straight line from the ladybug to

the aphid, you will see that the shortest path does not run down the edge.

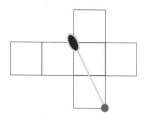

403

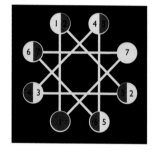

The key is to place each coin on a circle that is connected to the starting position of the previous coin. There will always be one pathway free, according to this strategy.

A more trial-and-error approach involves filling the star

with seven coins and playing the puzzle in reverse, noting the moves. You could also imagine untangling the star to form a circle, which would enable you to visualize the solution easily.

This puzzle offers an introduction to "clock arithmetic" and finite number systems. Its star track can be described as a modulus 8 with a linking operation of +3 (or −5). That is, there are eight points spaced around a circle, and every third point is joined to form a single continuous track.

404 Yellow and orange, red and green, pink and blue.

405 One of the small chains was separated into its three separate links, and then that was used to link together the other four chains.

406 Only the bottom left cube.

407 Regular tetrahedrons will not fill the space. When four pyramids are grouped together to define a larger tetrahedron, the central space is a regular octahedron.

Therefore, the pyramid is made up of eleven tetrahedrons and four octahedrons.

408 The minimal prismatic one-sided ring is made up of ten unit cubes.

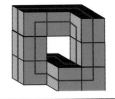

409 Numbers 2, 3, 4, 5 and 10 are identical. And numbers 7, 8 and 9 are identical. But number 1 and number 6 are unique.

410 If you hold a cube so that one corner points directly toward you, its edges outline a hexagon. It then becomes obvious that the cube has ample space for a square hole slightly larger than one of its faces.

If a cube has sides of 1 unit, a square hole can be drilled through it with sides of almost 1.06 units.

411 To solve this difficult problem in a systematic fashion, you can create a table that shows the number of different cubes possible for each combination of colors.

Number of red corners:
8 7 6 5 4 3 2 1 0

Number of yellow corners:
0 1 2 3 4 5 6 7 8

Number of different cubes:
1 1 3 3 7 3 3 1 1

Therefore, twenty-three different cubes are possible.

412 The green loop.

413 Only the yellow, green and orange nets can be folded into a perfect cube.

414

415 The sliced-off tetrahedron has one-sixth the volume of the whole box.

416 No path exists. The next best answer is a path that leaves one room unvisited.

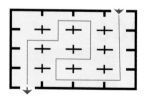

CHAPTER 12 SOLUTIONS

417 Yes. Weight is a relative magnitude, and your weight may change from planet to planet, but a spring scale will always be able to measure that weight—even though your weight will often be 0.

418 No. At the surface the moon's gravitational pull is only one-sixth that of the earth's, so astronauts on the moon will weigh only $\frac{1}{6}$ of what they did on the earth.

419 When I pull on the string from the bottom slowly and steadily, the top part of the string must bear both the weight of the book and the strength of the pull. The tension on it is greater than the tension on the lower half, so the top thread will break first.

If I pull with a sharp jerk, inertia comes into play. The book is little affected by the jerk at first, so the force of the jerk is not transmitted to the top string. The tension is therefore greater on the bottom thread and it breaks first.

420 The biggest and heaviest apples will rise to the top.

The arrangement that is most stable is one in which the most densely packed apples are at the bottom. The smaller an object is, the more likely it is to find a space to drop into at a lower position. Therefore, in a group of mixed apples, the smaller apples can be more densely packed than the large ones and will eventually sink to the bottom.

421 Whether large or small, packed spheres will occupy about .5235 cubic meters for every cubic meter of space they are packed in. This is independent of the size of the ball, as long as the radius is small in relation to the size of the box.

Even though each void is smaller for tightly packed small spheres, there are more voids altogether. Each box will weigh the same.

422 This thought experiment was devised by the great Albert Einstein and demonstrates his equivalence principle: The effect of being at rest in a gravitational field is the same as the effect of being at rest in an accelerated system.

If you are in an accelerating rocket as described, you will feel yourself pulled toward the floor with the same force—and watch objects fall at the same speed— as if you were in a room on the earth, though it is the floor that is actually rising up to meet the objects.

In the absence of other information, then, it is impossible to tell whether you are on the earth or in an accelerating rocket.

423 Common sense tells us that heavy objects should accelerate faster than lighter ones, but experimental science has proven this is not the case.

Newton's second law of motion shows that acceleration is directly proportional to force (weight, in this case) and inversely proportional to mass.

The equation can be written as:

$$a = f/m$$

where a is acceleration, f is force and m is mass.

The resistance to motion due to mass is called inertia. Therefore, even though a large stone may weigh 100 times more than a small rock, it has 100 times more mass (and inertia), and so the two factors cancel out.

In general, and ignoring air resistance, the acceleration of every falling body near sea level is 32 feet per second per second.

424

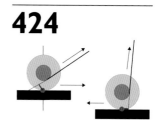

If you pull up at a sharp angle, a torque is created that turns the spool away from you. If you pull instead at a more shallow angle, the opposite torque is created, and the spool will roll toward you.

425 Friction will always keep the stick from falling. The finger that is farther from the stick's center of gravity carries a lighter load and therefore experiences less friction, so that finger moves first. As it is brought closer to the center, more and more weight is borne by that finger until the kinetic friction between the stick and the finger is greater than the static friction between the stick and the other finger. At that point the first finger stops and the second finger begins to slide. The stick will first slide over one finger, then on the other, switching back and forth until both fingers meet at the stick's center of gravity.

Starting from the middle, the finger that moves first immediately bears less weight and continues to bear less weight as it moves. There will be no alternating motion in this case.

426 The weight is the same in both instances. The weight depends on the mass of the bottle and its contents, and that does not change. When flies are in flight, their weight is transmitted to the bottle by air currents, especially the downdraft generated by moving wings.

427 Weigh three parcels against three parcels. If one side is heavier than the other side, one of those three must contain the ring. If both sides are equal, the ring must be in one of the three that were not weighed. From the group of three with the ring, weigh one against another. The heavier of the two has the ring; if both are equal, the ring will be found in the unweighed parcel.

428 The spout of the yellow can reaches to its rim and so may be filled completely. The green can, while taller, has a low spout and thus may be only partially filled. The yellow can will hold more.

429 Clockwise.

430 Start both timers simultaneously. When the three-minute timer ends, turn it over quickly. When the four-minute timer ends, turn the three-minute timer over once again—there will be one minute's worth of sand to add to the four minutes to make a full five minutes.

431 Clockwise.

432 When this paradox was first discovered, complex explanations were advanced to account for the hourglass's behavior. But its workings are quite simple.

When the cylinder is turned over, the hourglass's high center of gravity makes it topple over, and its buoyancy helps wedge the glass against the sides of the cylinder. Friction between glass and glass holds the hourglass in place until enough sand has passed to the lower compartment to drop the center of gravity. Only then will the hourglass free up and rise to the top.

433 If you throw your Frisbee with real gusto, it will travel all the way around the earth without falling. Since there is no friction from the air, it will continue to orbit without any need of additional propulsion. It will become a satellite.

The moon and communication satellites circle the earth in much the same way as the planets circle the sun.

434 Clockwise.

435 Both racks will move up.

436 To the left.

437 After 1 ¼ clockwise turns of the leftmost gear, the letters will spell out LEONARDO.

438 The bridge did not support the clown. Newton's third law of motion states that every action has an equal and opposite reaction; the clown applied a force to the rings to lift them into the air—a force that was greater than the weight of the rings. That force, plus the weight of the clown and the other ring, broke the bridge.

439 Mr. Smith should throw the Frisbee backward so that the dog will have to run the additional distance Mr. Smith walks while he retrieves the Frisbee.

440 Many people are boggled by this puzzle and try to sum up an infinite series straight out of advanced math. But the answer is simple: it takes the joggers an hour to meet, and the fly travels 10 kilometers in an hour.

In his fascinating book *Time Travel and Other Math Bewilderments*, Martin Gardner tells a story about the Hungarian mathematician John von Neumann, who was asked this puzzle at a party. Neumann gave the correct answer in an instant. The person who posed the question was disappointed;

he usually could count on mathematicians to overlook the obvious answer and try instead to solve the problem through the time-consuming process of summing up an infinite series.

Von Neumann was startled. "But that's how I solved it," he said.

441 The wheel with the weight at the center will arrive first. Because the weight is at the center, it will not resist turning as much as the weight placed near the rim. That means the wheel will speed up much more quickly. But the wheel that has the weight near the outside, though it doesn't speed up as quickly, will not slow down as quickly either: it will roll longer than the other wheel.

442 The trick works. There's more than gravity working on the bucket: the falling arm of the ladder has its center of mass near the pivot point because of the heavy weight. The resultant torque causes the end of the arm to descend faster than a free fall. As long as the bucket lands in the line of the falling bowling ball, the ball will land in the bucket.

443 The bottle must be dropped from a height four times as great.

Doubling the height seems intuitively sufficient. But to double the speed, one must double the time of the fall, which means that four times the potential energy must be put into the system.

444 The frog advances 1 meter a day. After seventeen full days the frog is 3 meters from the exit. The frog escapes on the eighteenth day.

445 Velocity is speed in a particular direction, so the velocity of the ball is constantly changing because its direction is constantly changing.

A change in velocity means acceleration. And the ball is accelerating toward the center of the circle. In fact, anything that moves in a circle accelerates toward the center of the circle. The acceleration changes the velocity just enough to make the ball follow the path of a circle.

If the string broke, the ball would move off in a straight line tangent to the circle at that point.

446 Golf balls always fly with backspin. The dimples trap a layer of air that spins the ball. The top layer of trapped air moves faster than the bottom layer, giving the ball greater lift. This is called Bernoulli's principle, which is also the basis of airplane flight.

A smooth golf ball would travel about half the distance that a dimpled golf ball can cover.

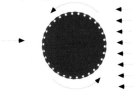

447 The stool—and the boy—will start rotating in the opposite direction. The angular momentum is conserved by having the two opposite rotations cancel out.

448 Nothing will happen! The response to the tire's angular momentum will try to drive the stool into the ground.

449 Surprisingly, the pendulums will not end up with the same amount of energy. Instead, energy will be periodically exchanged between them in such a way that sometimes one and sometimes the other of them stops.

As one of the pendulums is set in motion, after some time its energy will pass over to the other pendulum, which will gradually overtake the first swing. Eventually the first pendulum will be stationary. Then the whole procedure starts over again.

450

Place the glass over the marble and move it around so that the marble starts to spin around the inside of the glass. Once the marble starts rotating, it will begin to rise off the table. When the marble is spinning fast enough, you can lift the glass off the table. The marble will not drop immediately; it will continue to spin around under its own momentum.

451 The woodpecker is a simple mechanical oscillator. The hole in the ring around the vertical rod is slightly larger than the diameter of the stick. When the woodpecker is at rest, friction keeps the ring in place on the rod. But when it moves, the ring becomes vertical at the midpoint of each oscillation. Because the ring is now not wedged in place, it slips down a bit along the rod. This slight drop gives enough of a jolt to the bird to keep it vibrating. So at each drop, potential energy is converted into movement—kinetic energy.

The oscillating woodpecker also demonstrates the basic principle of a grandfather clock: the simple escape mechanism.

452 Suspended bodies tend to rotate around the axes of the greatest moment of inertia.

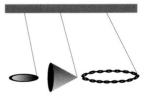

453 Pushing the handle forward with his right hand and backward with his left one will cause the wheel to tilt to the left.

As paradoxical as it may sound, to turn the stool, the boy must push upward on the right side of the handle and down on the left side. He will then feel the gyroscopic precession: the property of the axis of a spinning body to resist a tilting force by moving in a direction at right angle to that force. The bicycle wheel, which is no different from a gyroscope, resists the tilting force, and its axis begins to rotate at a right angle to what one might expect. The turn of the wheel to the left is transferred to the revolving stool with the boy.

A turning wheel resists any change in speed and direction. Unless you push it in some specific way, the wheel will keep spinning in the same direction. If you turn it, it tilts. If you tilt it, it turns.

Indeed, any fast-spinning object will act like a gyroscope—bicycle and motorcycle riders often experience gyroscopic effects.

454 The skater will spin much faster. By bringing her arms to her chest, she decreases the moment of inertia of her body because more of her weight is now concentrated near the center. To compensate for this, there is an increase in her angular velocity. If the spin becomes too fast for her, she can stretch her arms back out to slow down.

All moving objects have energy of movement, or kinetic energy. The kinetic energy stored by something spinning depends on two things: the way its weight is distributed and how fast it spins.

Flywheels utilize this idea, though in the opposite way. They are designed to store as much energy as possible when they spin. Most of their weight, therefore, is concentrated near the rim.

455 The centripetal force caused by the rotating cylinder is perpendicular to the wall, creating friction. When the circular acceleration is high enough, the friction force can overcome the force of gravity and prevent the carnival riders from falling when the floor is removed.

456 Since the lines radiating from John's shot are the source for the others that branch off from them, John was first.

457 It takes longer to drop than to fly up.
The ball has to work against air resistance on its way up and so continuously loses energy. Thus, the total energy of a ball at a point on its way up is greater than its energy at the same height on its way down. Since the potential energy (its energy due to its height) is the same at both instances, the difference in energy must be due to a reduced kinetic energy. That means the falling ball is moving more slowly and will take more time to cover the same distance.

458 Every dimension of the washer will expand, so the hole will get larger too.

459 The branching pattern is more economical than the radial pattern. The branching pattern has a much shorter total length than the radial pattern, at the expense of only a slightly longer average path length. Thus, trees, blood vessels, rivers and even subway networks are all examples of branching patterns.

460 The balls will actually move toward each other. The air moving between the balls has a lower pressure than the surrounding air, which pushes the two balls together.
This is a simple demonstration of the Bernoulli's principle, which links air speed and air pressure. This is also the basis of airplane flight.

461 According to Archimedes' principle, an object floats because it displaces an amount of water equal to the weight of the object. So to float when the ring was placed on it, the duck must displace a volume of water that equals the weight of the ring.

Since the metal ring is denser than water, the volume of the displaced water is greater than the volume of the ring. When the ring falls in the water and sinks, it displaces only its own volume of water.

The water level, then, drops when the ring slips off the duck and into the tub.

462 The wings of an airplane are designed so that air will rush across their upper surface faster than it rushes past the lower surface. For this reason the top surface of the wings is made longer than the bottom.

As described in Bernoulli's principle, that extra speed lowers the pressure above the wings, producing a net force from below called lift. That force keeps the airplane in the air as it moves forward. When an airplane is in midflight, the combined weight of the plane, fuel, passengers and cargo exerts a heavy pull downward. However, that total weight is overcome by the lift, allowing the airplane to remain airborne.

463 Rapidly moving air has low pressure, and a column of upward-rushing air can actually imprison a lightweight object like a Ping-Pong ball. As soon as the ball wobbles a bit to one side, the greater pressure outside of the airstream forces the ball back to the middle.

464 The lightweight Ping-Pong ball will rise very quickly in still water.

But when the water is agitated, the buoyancy of the ball is drastically reduced. The movement of the liquid produces higher pressures that make the displacement of the water by the ball more difficult.

465 The stream of air creates a low-pressure area, drawing the flames together.

466 As tricky as the problem sounds, there is exactly the same amount of milk in the tea as there is tea in the milk. As you can see in the diagram above, the total volume in each glass is unchanged by the transfer; the net volume transferred from glass A to glass B exactly cancels that which went from glass B to glass A.

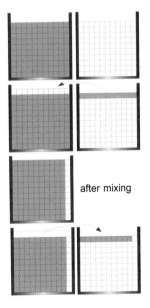

after mixing

467 Large raindrops fall faster.

A falling drop is subject to two opposing forces—gravity and air resistance. Air resistance is proportional to the drop's cross section, and it increases with velocity. At first, the slowing effect of air resistance is very small, and the drop keeps falling faster because of the constant force of gravity. As the speed increases, so does air resistance—until the speed is so great that the force of air resistance equally opposes the force of gravity. From that point the drop starts falling at a uniform speed, the so-called terminal velocity.

The force of gravity grows in proportion to the drop's volume, which is the cube of the radius. On the other hand, air resistance builds up at the cross-section area of the drop, which is the square of the radius. As the drop's radius increases, the force of gravity increases faster than the opposing force of air resistance. The drop can reach a greater terminal velocity before the air resistance catches up with it.

468 The water level will stay exactly as before.

The weight of the water displaced by the iceberg exactly equals the weight of the iceberg. When the iceberg melts, it turns back into water and fills the volume of water it displaced.

The volume of the iceberg above the water must exactly equal the increased volume of the water that froze and expanded to become ice.

469 The air pressure at the moving end of the tube is lower than the pressure at the end being held. That pressure difference causes the air to flow through the tube, and the air vibrates as it passes over the corrugated walls of the tube.

470 When you stick your finger in the water, your finger takes the place of some of the water, and so the water level goes up.

Your finger not only takes the place of some of the water but also stands in for the weight of that water. The glass weighs more, by the weight of that displaced water. The weight of the object displacing the water is not a factor; it could be a balloon or a lead cylinder.

471

Fill the glass with water until it forms a convex lip above the rim. Then place the cork in the glass. The cork will seek the highest point, which is now in the middle, and stay there.

472 The magnification will actually decrease.

The amount by which a lens can bend rays of light depends on both the curvature of the glass and the difference in the speed of light between air and glass. The difference in speed from water to glass is less than that between air and glass, so the lens will not bend the light as powerfully and therefore will not magnify the image as much.

473 The last time I tried this, I was able to add fifty-two pennies to a supposedly full cup of water before it overflowed.

Water has a high surface tension. It behaves as though it had a flexible skin on its surface; that skin pulls inward and resists breaking. Not only can a glass of water develop a great bulge before it flows over the edge of the container, but the surface tension can support the weight of light objects. If you place a clean razor blade flat against the surface of a glass of water, the blade can actually "float"—not because of buoyancy but because of the support of surface tension.

474

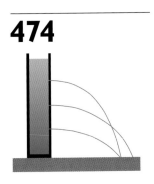

The distance the water will squirt depends on the exit speed of the water out of the hole multiplied by the time it takes the water to reach the table. The middle hole has the greatest range because speed increases with the square root of the water depth (because of water pressure), while time increases with the square root of the distance to the surface. This product is highest at the halfway point.

475 Because the sun is so large, the shadow will be smaller, but the difference in size is imperceptible. But if the sun is at an angle to the shadow surface, such as an hour or less before sunset, the shadow can be much larger.

Light rays from a distant object may appear parallel, but this is not necessarily the case. If the light source is larger than the object, the shadow (on a flat surface perpendicular to the light source) will be smaller. If the light source is smaller than the object, then the shadow will be larger. The difference in size, however, is scarcely perceptible if the distance between the two objects is great.

476 The angle will remain 15 degrees. Some measurements do not change when dimensions are magnified.

477 One way to route the light rays is shown; ten mirrors have been rotated.

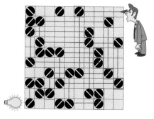

478 It doesn't matter how far you are from the mirror, as long as it is hung at the correct height—with the lower edge at half the height of the eyes of the person looking in the mirror.

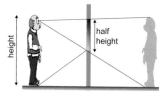

479 Three meters. The image of the flower in the hand mirror is as far behind that mirror as the flower is in front of it: .5 meter. That puts the image of the flower .5 + .5 + 2, or 3 meters, in front of the large mirror, so that is the distance behind the large mirror that its reflected image forms.

CHAPTER 13 SOLUTIONS

480 The design shown below requires only twelve outlets.

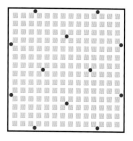

481 It is problematic to solve this sort of problem by looking at the three-dimensional figure; some corners and edges will always be hidden. Instead, one can create a topologically equivalent two-dimensional diagram, such as this one, on which to work out the solution.

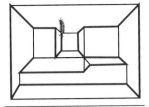

482 For whichever of the seven horses comes in first, there are six different horses that can come in second; for each of the forty-two different combinations of first- and second-place horses, there are five different horses that can come in third. That means there are 7 × 6 × 5, or 210, different combinations of horses.

483

A circle can be divided into any number of regions of equal area using a compass and a ruler. Simply divide the diameter into the number of equal divisions required and from those points draw semicircles, as shown.

Ancient Chinese mathematicians knew of this method; the yin-yang is an example.

484 To take into account the worst possible scenario (five red, five yellow, five green and one blue), you must grab sixteen wires.

485 The results are independent of the way the smaller shapes intrude on the larger. After all, the overlap is removed from both the red and blue areas. Therefore, one easy method for comparing the red and blue areas is to find the difference between the sum of the areas of the smaller shapes and the area of the largest shape.

Circles ($r^2\pi$):
Red and blue areas are equal.

Squares (a^2):
Blue area is larger.

Triangles ($a^2/4\sqrt{3}$):
Sum of the red areas is larger.

486 The number of nonrepeating three-letter combinations are

26 × 25 × 24, or 15,600

That means his chances are .0064 percent.

487 There must be at least two such boys.

488 There are fifteen unique pairs of dogs. If the dogs are named, say, A, B, C, D, E and F, the possible pairs are: AB, AC, AD, AE, AF, BC, BD, BE, BF, CD, CE, CF, DE, DF and EF.

489 These sixteen combinations of four numbers are part of a larger set of eighty-six possible combinations of numbers from 1 through 16 that total 34.

490 The answer can be found by simple multiplication: $26 \times 10 \times 10 \times 10 \times 26 \times 26 \times 26$, or 456,976,000.

491 The eight groups represent the eight possible ways to create different triplets of the numbers 1 through 9 that add up to 15.

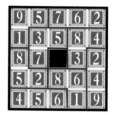

492 Only three colors are necessary, as shown.

493 Four colors are needed, as shown.

494 Each spot on the robot's electronic display can either show 1, 2, 3 or be blank. That means it can show three different one-digit numbers:

1, 2, 3

nine different two-digit numbers:

11, 12, 13, 21, 22, 23, 31, 32, 33,

and twenty-seven different three-digit numbers:

111, 112, 113, 121, 122, 123, 131, 132, 133, 211, 212, 213, 221, 222, 223, 231, 232, 233, 311, 312, 313, 321, 322, 323, 331, 332, 333

for a total of thirty-nine numbers. You can solve this easily with this formula:

$$3 + 3^2 + 3^3 = 39$$

495 This is a classic game, here in a form suggested by Peter Gabor. There are six *F*s. The *F*s in *of* are easy to overlook.

496 The Pythagorean theorem ensures that the areas are exactly equal. Two radii of a pair of touching quarter circles are at right angles to each other, and the radius of the matching quarter circle

stretches across the hypotenuse, completing the right triangle.

497 This sequence of numbers details the number of new pairs of rabbits produced each month, starting with the first new pair born in January. The total number of pairs is 376.

Jan	Feb	Mar	Apr	May	Jun
1	1	2	3	5	8

Jul	Aug	Sep	Oct	Nov	Dec
13	21	34	55	89	144

498 The total number of soldiers plus the general must be a square number. The smallest square that is also equal to 1 plus a multiple of eleven is 100, which is $9 \times 11 + 1$.

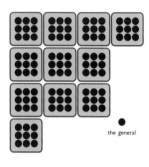

the general

499

500 The general answer to this problem, called the hailstone problem because of the way the numbers cycle in much the same way as hailstones growing in a thundercloud, is not known. But none of the numbers up to 26 survive for long. Beginning with 7, you get:

7, 22, 11, 34, 17, 52,
26, 13, 40, 20, 10, 5, 16,
8, 4, 2, 1, and so on

The number 27 takes an interesting journey, making it up to 9,232 at step 77 before crashing. It reaches the 1-4-2-1-4-2 loop in step 111. Every number up to a trillion has been tested, and every one eventually collapses into the rut.

501 The answer is simple: the young man should simply ask, "Are you married?"

Regardless of who answers his question, he knows that a "yes" means that Amelia is married and a "no" means Leila is married. Virtuous Amelia will tell him the truth—"yes" if she is, "no" if Leila is—no matter what, and wicked Leila will say "no" if she is married and "yes" if she is single and Amelia is married.

502

You simply move each guest into the room with the number that is twice that of the room he or she is in now. The person in room 1 goes to room 2, the person in room 2 goes to room 4, the person in room 3 goes to room 6 and so on. All the odd-numbered rooms will be vacated, and since there are an infinite number of odd numbers, all your new guests can be accommodated.

503

You should ask him, "Which way to your hometown?"

If he is from Truth City, he'll point to it; if he is from Lies City, he will also point to Truth City.

504

The largest sum you can see on any given die is 15, that is, the sum of 4, 5 and 6. Therefore, the only possible combinations of three different numbers that total 40 are 15 + 14 + 11 and 15 + 13 + 12. But a sum of 13 is impossible to see on the three faces of a real die. (Try it if you doubt this.) That leaves

the only answer as 15, 14 and 11, as shown.

505

When two six-sided dice are thrown against each other, there are thirty-six possible outcomes. The table below shows the results of die C versus die D: C wins twenty-four times, D wins just twelve. Similar results can be found with D versus A, A versus B, and B versus C. No matter what die your opponent selects, you can pick the die to its immediate left (or D if your opponent chooses A) and win two out of every three times.

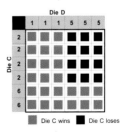

506 You should ask, "Am I in Las Wages?" and "Am I in Las Wages?"

Two yeses will come from a truth teller; two nos from a liar. And a yes and a no will mean that the person alternated between truth and lie.

---

507 The structure is made up of two separate pieces and could be pulled apart.

---

508 Although the coin has an equal chance of landing on heads after every throw, the player who tosses first has a decided advantage, no matter how long the game lasts. The probability that the first player will win is the sum of the probabilities that occur at every turn:

$$\tfrac{1}{2} + (\tfrac{1}{2})^3 + (\tfrac{1}{2})^5 + (\tfrac{1}{2})^7 + \dots$$

This is a series with an infinite number of terms that approaches two-thirds in value. Therefore, the player who tosses first has a chance of winning that is almost twice that of the second player. If you are surprised at this result, play a number of games and keep track of who comes out on top.

---

509 The diagram shows all the possible orientations, starting with point 1. As you can see, a right triangle is formed eighteen out of twenty-one times, which means the probability is $\tfrac{6}{7}$.

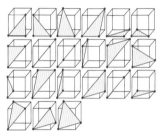

---

510 In fact, the Pythagorean theorem is valid not only for hexagons and squares but for any set of geometrically similar figures.

Schmerl found a five-piece solution to his problem (shown below, left and right) and American mathematician Greg Frederickson found a "sneaky" four-piece solution. Both are shown.

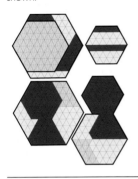

511 There are 21 possible pairs among seven birds. You can use such a list to systematically work out a foraging schedule:

Day 1: 1, 2, 3, involving the pairs 1-2, 1-3 and 2-3

Day 2: 1, 4, 5, involving the pairs 1-4, 1-5 and 4-5

Day 3: 1, 6, 7, involving the pairs 1-6, 1-7 and 6-7

Day 4: 2, 4, 6, involving the pairs 2-4, 2-6 and 4-6

Day 5: 2, 5, 7, involving the pairs 2-5, 2-7 and 5-7

Day 6: 3, 4, 7, involving the pairs 3-4, 3-7 and 4-7

Day 7: 3, 5, 6, involving the pairs 3-5, 3-6 and 5-6

512 The minimal path is a tree—a graph with no closed loops—on which lines are joined together at angles of 120 degrees to one another. For large numbers of points, it is difficult to predict the minimal path. Interestingly, though, a three-dimensional model immersed in a soapy solution will give the solution for even the most complex configurations in an instant.

The five-town solution was provided by Nick Baxter.

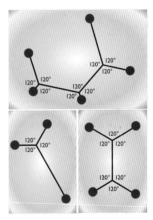

513

514

There is less than a 2 percent chance:

$\frac{6}{6} \times \frac{5}{6} \times \frac{4}{6} \times \frac{3}{6} \times \frac{2}{6} \times \frac{1}{6} = 0.015$,

or 1.5 percent

515

In the linked tubes, the water level will be the same. Pressure is independent of the volume or shape of the tube and depends only on the height of the liquid. This is called the hydrostatic paradox.

516

The eleventh square will have sides of 32 units. For every two steps in the progression, the length of the sides doubles.

517

There are exactly eight possibilities for the product of three ages to be 36:

Son 1	Son 2	Son 3	Product	Sum
1	1	36	36	38
1	2	18	36	21
1	3	12	36	16
1	4	9	36	14
1	6	6	36	13
2	2	9	36	13
2	3	6	36	11
3	3	4	36	10

Since Ivan could not solve the problem when he knew the sum of the three numbers—the date of the encounter—that meant the sum must have been 13, for which there are two possibilities. The added information about the youngest son means that one of the possibilities—a nine-year-old and two two-year-olds—can be ruled out, since there is no one youngest son in that case.

That left Ivan with one solution: 1, 6 and 6.

NOTES

NOTES